Simplifying State Management in React Native

Master state management from hooks and context through to Redux, MobX, XState, Jotai and React Query

Aleksandra Desmurs-Linczewska

BIRMINGHAM—MUMBAI

Simplifying State Management in React Native

Group Product Manager: Rohit Rajkumar
Publishing Product Manager: Nitin Nainani
Senior Editor: Aamir Ahmed
Technical Editor: Joseph Aloocaran
Copy Editor: Safis Editing
Project Coordinator: Manthan Patel
Proofreader: Safis Editing
Indexer: Rekha Nair
Production Designer: Ponraj Dhandapani
Marketing Coordinator: Nivedita Pandey

First published: January 2023

Production reference: 1081222

Published by Packt Publishing Ltd.
Livery Place
35 Livery Street
Birmingham
B3 2PB, UK.

ISBN 978-1-80323-503-5

www.packt.com

To my entire family, for supporting me throughout the process of writing this book.

– Aleksandra Desmurs-Linczewska

Contributors

About the author

Aleksandra Desmurs-Linczewska is a web and software developer with experience reaching as far as Flash and websites laid out with tables. Aleks has seen her fair share of diverse code bases, bugs, and Jira tickets. She studied French literature, but after graduating, she decided to opt for a career in IT, which has always interested her. She started out creating websites for friends and family. Soon, she landed her first paying job at a software house in Sopot, Poland. A few years later, she learned about React Native and started writing her first app back in 2018. She's been working on both React JS and React Native since then. However, she strongly favors React Native. She personally published a weather app, and she participates in OSS projects and helps out with PRs, issues, and discussions. She recently started working for Callstack, the biggest React Native software house in Poland.

I want to thank my family – for understanding how much time writing a book can take. I'd also like to thank my team at Packt, for being so understanding of how long it took me to write this book. I would especially like to thank Inderpal, who found me and convinced me to try this, and Aamir for his never-ending patience toward me and his tireless work.

About the reviewers

Piyush Nanwani is an IT professional with three years of experience as a full-stack developer and has worked on designing, developing, and deploying software applications. Powered by his passion for technology, he has delivered more than six production-ready self-started projects. Currently, he is working as a mobile app developer with M/s. Atlantis Intelligence Ltd. A recent project of his was developing a low-code platform to build mobile apps. Currently, he is working on React Native, React JS, MS SQL, and .NET, among other things. He holds a B.Tech degree in computer science from IP University, New Delhi.

His interests include exploring new technologies, attending conferences, reading books, and dancing.

You can reach Piyush at `https://www.linkedin.com/in/piiyush`.

Ahir Jere is an experienced full-stack developer. He has worked with a variety of platforms, such as embedded systems and desktop and mobile applications, as well as cloud applications. Well-versed in Python and JavaScript, he has multiple applications powered by Django and Node.js and creates beautiful, vibrant UI applications with React and Flutter. These applications range from art galleries for showcasing peoples' photography to large e-commerce stores with a wide variety of products and banking applications for different FinTech applications.

Table of Contents

Part 2 – Creating a Real, Working App

3

4

Part 3 – Exploring Various Libraries for State Management in React Native

5

6

Using MobX as a State Manager in a React Native App   101

7

Untangling Complex Flows in React Native Apps with XState   119

8

Integrating Jotai in a React Native App   141

9

Part 4 – Summary

10

Preface

Welcome to the wonderful world of React Native apps! Thanks to this technology, you can have your own native app up and running in a matter of minutes. Don't worry if this is the first time you are hearing about React Native. Basic knowledge of JavaScript will be enough to hit the ground running. Together, we will go over the important concepts of React and React Native and we will learn about the React Native ecosystem, setup, and tooling. By the end of *Chapter 4, Styling and Populating the Funbook App*, you will have a fully functioning social-media clone app in your hands.

This is where stuff starts getting interesting. Our app has a few API endpoints and needs to manage data objects across multiple components and screens. This situation is very common in medium-sized and large applications. Because of this, there are many solutions to this common problem. A lot of developers use battle-tested and renowned open-source libraries, such as Redux or MobX. Others look for innovative ideas and land on XState or Jotai for their projects. Others still use built-in React functionalities or concentrate on data fetching instead of state management with the help of React Query. Throughout this book, we will put ourselves in the shoes of all of these types of developers. We will pick one specific functionality from the app – the like button with the list of liked images – and we will try out the open source libraries listed here, one by one.

When we emerge victorious at the end of this book, you will have a very good understanding of different ways to manage states in React Native apps. I hope you will also have an idea of what you prefer, and why. Redux, MobX, XState, Jotai, and React Query were created to solve the same problem, but their creators approached it very differently. I also hope you will simply enjoy this book as much as I've enjoyed writing it.

Who this book is for

This book is meant for beginners in the React and React Native world. It covers basic topics pertinent to software development with ReactJS. Even if you are knowledgeable about basic React solutions, you may be a newbie to MobX, XState, Jotai, or React Query, which means this book is meant for you as well.

What this book covers

Chapter 1, What are React and React Native?, will start by going over a brief history of web development to achieve a better understanding of the ideas behind the creation of React and React Native. We will also talk about ReactJS concepts, and we will get acquainted with React Native code.

Chapter 2, Managing State in a Simple React App, will talk about some real-life problems that React developers face. We will concentrate on robust state management for medium-sized and large applications. Since React itself was not created with the tools to manage global states, we will look at modern React solutions and other state management strategies.

Chapter 3, Planning and Setting Up the Funbook App, will get into coding for real here! We will create our very own app, a social media clone app, called Funbook. We will learn about popular tools, especially Expo, and the React Native ecosystem.

Chapter 4, Styling and Populating the Funbook App, will be all about making the app we have on our hands look good. We will also populate it with some data so that we can work on a project that's close to how a real production app may work.

Chapter 5, Implementing Redux in Our Funbook App, will explore the tumultuous history of Redux and then go over configuring Redux and Redux Toolkit in the app. Once the dependencies are set up, we will move on to implementing the like button and the list of liked images with the help of Redux. This chapter includes responses from a short conversation I had with the main Redux and Redux Toolkit maintainer – Mark Erikson, also known by his Twitter handle @acemarke.

Chapter 6, Using MobX as a State Manager in a React Native App, will return to the bare React Native app we created in *Chapters 1* to *4*, and this time, we will add MobX and MobX-State-Tree into the mix. We will start with how this library came to be, and then move on to configuring it in the Funbook app. Once we're ready, we will use it for the liked images list and the like button. This chapter includes responses from an exchange I had with the MobX-State-Tree maintainer – Jamon Holmgren.

Chapter 7, Untangling Complex Flows in React Native Apps with XState, will go deeper into some advanced math problems, as XState is based on advanced mathematical concepts. When we have a handle on them, we will move on to configuring XState in the Funbook app and using it for the liked images functionality.

This chapter includes responses I received from the creator of XState – David Khourshid, better known on the internet as DavidKPiano.

Chapter 8, Integrating Jotai in a React Native App, will return to the bare Funbook app again, and this time, we will implement the youngest state management library in this book: Jotai. We will learn about its concepts, configure it, and use it for the liked button and liked images list functionality. This chapter includes responses from a conversation I had with the creator of Jotai, Daishi Kato.

Chapter 9, Using React Query for Server-Side - Driven State Management, will look at the problem of state management in a very new way: maybe we don't need state management libraries at all. Maybe all we must do is effectively manage data fetching. In order to test this hypothesis, we will install, configure, and use React Query, also known as TanStack Query.

Chapter 10, Appendix, will take a bird's eye view of everything that we have learned about in the book. I have also included a few common job interview questions that are pertinent to the topic of state management in React Native apps.

To get the most out of this book

You will need to install Expo on your computer. All code examples have been tested using Expo 44 on macOS, but they should work with future version releases.

Software/hardware covered in the book	Operating system requirements
Expo 44	Windows, macOS, or Linux
JavaScript (ECMAScript 2020)	Windows, macOS, or Linux
ReactJS v18 and up	Windows, macOS, or Linux
React Native	Windows, macOS, or Linux

Additional setup instructions are detailed in *Chapter 3, Planning and Setting Up the Funbook App*.

If you are using the digital version of this book, we advise you to type the code yourself or access the code from the book's GitHub repository (a link is available in the next section). Doing so will help you avoid any potential errors related to the copying and pasting of code.

This book represents the state of the most well-known state management libraries in 2022. I encourage you to try new and lesser-known solutions on your own, as new libraries are published every day.

Download the example code files

You can download the example code files for this book from GitHub at `https://github.com/PacktPublishing/Simplifying-State-Management-in-React-Native`. If there's an update to the code, it will be updated in the GitHub repository.

We also have other code bundles from our rich catalog of books and videos available at `https://github.com/PacktPublishing/`. Check them out!

Download the color images

We also provide a PDF file that has color images of the screenshots and diagrams used in this book. You can download it here: `https://packt.link/wv4Mk`.

Conventions used

There are a number of text conventions used throughout this book.

`Code in text`: Indicates code words in text, database table names, folder names, filenames, file extensions, pathnames, dummy URLs, user input, and Twitter handles. Here is an example: "export const ListOfAvatars = () => {".

A block of code is set as follows:

```
Import { Text } from 'react-native';

const Welcome = () => {
  return <Text>Hello, World! </Text>;
}
```

When we wish to draw your attention to a particular part of a code block, the relevant lines or items are set in bold:

```
return (
    <View style={{ paddingTop: 30 }}>
      <FlatList
        data={arrayOfAvatars}
        renderItem={renderItem}
        keyExtractor={(item) => item.id}
      />
    </View>
```

Any command-line input or output is written as follows:

```
$ yarn add react-query
$ expo start
```

Bold: Indicates a new term, an important word, or words that you see onscreen. For instance, words in menus or dialog boxes appear in **bold**. Here is an example: "If you want to see your app on your phone, you'll find the **QR code** to scan in the **Expo Go app** right here. "

> **Browsing through sample data**
> You can see the example data used in the app whenever you'd like.

Get in touch

Feedback from our readers is always welcome.

General feedback: If you have questions about any aspect of this book, email us at customercare@ packtpub.com and mention the book title in the subject of your message.

Errata: Although we have taken every care to ensure the accuracy of our content, mistakes do happen. If you have found a mistake in this book, we would be grateful if you would report this to us. Please visit www.packtpub.com/support/errata and fill in the form.

Piracy: If you come across any illegal copies of our works in any form on the internet, we would be grateful if you would provide us with the location address or website name. Please contact us at copyright@packt.com with a link to the material.

If you are interested in becoming an author: If there is a topic that you have expertise in and you are interested in either writing or contributing to a book, please visit authors.packtpub.com.

Share Your Thoughts

Once you've read *Simplifying State Management in React Native*, we'd love to hear your thoughts! Scan the QR code below to go straight to the Amazon review page for this book and share your feedback.

https://packt.link/r/1-803-23503-9

Your review is important to us and the tech community and will help us make sure we're delivering excellent quality content.

Download a free PDF copy of this book

Thanks for purchasing this book!

Do you like to read on the go but are unable to carry your print books everywhere?

Is your eBook purchase not compatible with the device of your choice?

Don't worry, now with every Packt book you get a DRM-free PDF version of that book at no cost.

Read anywhere, any place, on any device. Search, copy, and paste code from your favorite technical books directly into your application.

The perks don't stop there, you can get exclusive access to discounts, newsletters, and great free content in your inbox daily

Follow these simple steps to get the benefits:

1. Scan the QR code or visit the link below

https://packt.link/free-ebook/978-1-80323-503-5

2. Submit your proof of purchase

3. That's it! We'll send your free PDF and other benefits to your email directly

Part 1 – Learn the Basics: Intro to React, States, Props, Hooks, and Context

In this part, we will start with some theoretical knowledge that will be vital for creating a real app. The Readers will learn some of the history of React and its general rules, guidelines, and best practices. Next, we will look into React's built-in strategies for dealing with states: local states, props, hooks, and context.

This part includes the following chapters:

- *Chapter 1, What are React and React Native?*
- *Chapter 2, Managing State in a Simple React App*

1

What are React and React Native?

Welcome to the magical world of **React** and **React Native**. I hope to make you feel at home here. It's okay if this is your very first contact with these frameworks, or you may have played around with them a little bit already. This book will focus on **managing state** in **React Native apps**, but we will start by going over the basics.

If React and React Native were people, the first one would be the parent of the second one. You can focus on the child framework, but you will find great benefits in getting to know the "parent" of React Native – **ReactJS**.

We will start this journey by going over the history of ReactJS and specifically, why it was created. We will then continue our study of ReactJS by looking into what it means to *think in React* or to have the *React mindset*. Once we're familiar with ReactJS, we will try to understand what **cross-platform software development** means and what place React Native holds in the cross-platform development ecosystem. For understanding the ecosystem, we will concentrate on React Native itself, its brief history, and its current state. We will finish our tour with a handful of examples of native apps written in React Native.

In this chapter, we will cover the following topics:

- Understanding the history of ReactJS
- Thinking in React (the React mindset)
- Understanding cross-platform software development
- Going over the history of React Native
- Reviewing examples of popular apps using React Native

By the end of this chapter, you will have high-level knowledge of React and React Native. You will also understand their place in the software development ecosystem.

Understanding the history of ReactJS

In this section, we will briefly look into the history of ReactJS. If you're not interested in this particular topic, feel free to skip this section and go straight to *Thinking in React*. Knowing the history of a framework is not compulsory for using it. If you prefer condensed knowledge served in a YouTube pill, I highly recommend watching a 10-minute video called *The Story of React*, published on YouTube by *uidotdev*.

The predecessors

Did you know that the first website ever created is still live? You can find it here: `http://info.cern.ch/hypertext/WWW/TheProject.html`. It was created in 1991! A lot has changed since then. For starters, web developers wanted to change their websites' appearance, hence CSS was created. A few years later those same web developers wanted to see more interactivity on their now beautiful websites. This is when **JavaScript** found its place on the internet. But as we know, the web never stops evolving. Heavy usage of JavaScript led to the creation of libraries such as jQuery, BackboneJS, and Ember. Each library's creators learned lessons from their competitors. They made decisions that led to creating very different developer experiences. The developers had their preferences and little wars over which library is better.

There is no right answer to this question. What is certain, however, is that user experience on websites evolved, no matter which library was used behind the scenes. Websites became much more interactive and adaptable to the user's screen size. For example, it is common practice today to create separate menus for mobile views and desktop views. This can be achieved with JavaScript, or CSS alone. This user experience shift could not take place without the evolution of JavaScript **open source** libraries.

After a few years of adding more and more separate bits of JavaScript to websites, it was time for a more holistic solution. The first breakthrough came from Google, with **AngularJS**. AngularJS, officially released in 2010, was different from other solutions on the market at that time. This was not just another library; this was a framework. Developers were able to create complex interactions quickly, and they were no longer afraid that any change to their JavaScript files could break the entire page. I don't want to go into the implementational details of AngularJS. After all, that is not the focus of this book. In broad strokes, AngularJS introduced special HTML attributes that were observed by the framework running in the background. As you may imagine, when JavaScript is observing dozens or even hundreds of elements and events, it will slow down. So, the user experience is suffering, and the world is ready for another JavaScript revolution. Google thought they would remain king of the hill with their Angular version 2, but in 2013, Facebook developers announced the release of ReactJS.

And then there was React

ReactJS was presented specifically as a **user interface (UI)** library. It was conceived to be used for end user interactions on websites. It also used **JSX** – an extension to JavaScript created for React. Many developers reacted, pun intended, angrily to this new syntax. I would say though, that angry reactions are not unexpected in the world of tech. Any new technological solution has to weather the storm of angry Reddit posts saying that it's ugly, useless, or simply terrible. Luckily for us, ReactJS developers did not stop working on their open source framework because of this initial negative reaction. Furthermore, developers who got to know ReactJS became its advocates. Why, you may ask, did ReactJS stand the test of time, while Angular hasn't? I believe it has to do with the high-level mindset of the framework. ReactJS proposes elegant, simple solutions while staying completely configurable to any needs. I will go further into this mindset idea in the next section.

Going back to our history lesson! We're in 2013, and ReactJS has entered the scene with a bang. Many people hate it, but others use it for more and more complex websites. And it turns out, unfortunately, that ReactJS does not scale well. Your React components use state and props. If the parent creates a state, which needs to be read four to five components lower in the hierarchy, you encounter something that is dubbed **prop drilling**. Prop drilling means that the developer has to pass the necessary prop through many parent components in order to get to the final child that needs to read it. This process is irritating and boring, at the same time! This is when the first state management library was created – **Redux**. We will talk in detail about Redux and other state management libraries in the next chapters.

As of writing this book, ReactJS is one of the most popular JavaScript libraries. It evolves constantly, and its maintainers are open to public discussions and suggestions. In 2019, they introduced hooks and context. These two React utilities can cover a lot of your state management needs. They were created because the React team realized that developers using React needed an improvement in the state management area.

A few years before the introduction of hooks and context, specifically in 2015, Facebook developers released React Native. The true hero of this book! But let's not get ahead of ourselves. At this moment, it is important that you understand the basic concepts of React. Let's move on to the React mindset.

Thinking in React (the React mindset)

The official ReactJS docs include a chapter called *Thinking in React*: `https://reactjs.org/docs/getting-started.html#thinking-in-react`.

> **Important note**
> Many React users credit reading *Thinking in React* (`https://reactjs.org/docs/thinking-in-react.html`) as the moment React finally clicked for them. It's probably the oldest React walk-through but it's still just as relevant.

Let's try and capture the most important, and still relevant, parts of that article.

First of all, when we create a website with ReactJS, we need to think about how we will construct our components. Not HTML blocks, not DOM elements, but components. Ideally, each component will be a separate entity, which either creates a state or consumes props, or sometimes both. The component is the smallest part of our app, just like atoms are the smallest parts of our world.

Okay, I realize atoms can be further divided into neutrons, protons, and electrons. And **ReactJS components** can be divided into parts that handle the logic and the actual rendering. However, both atoms and ReactJS components are the basic building blocks in their respective realms.

Now that we have our components imagined, we need to know how they should interact with each other. Let's go back to the ReactJS docs, where we will find a great chapter, *Composition vs. Inheritance*: https://reactjs.org/docs/composition-vs-inheritance.html.

This article is very clear in stating that ReactJS components should be composed, and not stacked in a strict hierarchy. This basically means that any child component should be created in a way that it could be reused by other parent components throughout the app. This promotes the high reusability of atomic components, and at the same time, reduces the amount of code needed to create an application.

Now that we have the theory down, let's move on to specifics. How do we compose ReactJS components in practice? By using state and props. What are those, you may ask? Well, I'll be glad to explain!

Both **state** and **props** (short for properties) are plain JavaScript objects. The big difference between them is that props are read-only, while state can be changed within the component that manages it. State is the source of truth, while props are the representations of the current state of the application. Let's take a look at a minimal code example:

```
import React, { useState } from "react";

const PrettyButton = ({ updateCount, count }) => {
  return (
      <button onClick={updateCount}>This was clicked {count} of
        times</button>
  );
};

export default function App() {
  const [counter, updateCount] = useState(0);

  const handleClick = () => {
    updateCount(counter + 1);
  };
```

```
  return (
    <div>
      <h1>Hello There!</h1>
        <PrettyButton count={counter} updateCount={handleClick}
          />
    </div>
  );
}
```

You can play with this sample code online thanks to this CodeSandbox: `https://codesandbox.io/s/admiring-fire-68k94x?file=/src/App.js`.

From the preceding code example, you can see that the App component creates the counter state, and the function responsible for updating it. `PrettyButton` consumes this state in the form of props. `PrettyButton` cannot change the value of `counter` or `updateCounter` directly.

If we were to write another parent component that needed to use `PrettyButton`, it would need to create its own `counter` and `updateCounter` states. And thanks to that, every instance of `PrettyButton` we may want to use in our web app will be independent of the others.

We may also find ourselves importing multiple child components in the main App component. This is totally natural. We may have an app with a button, a text, and a modal, all of which need to display the number of times the button was clicked. All we need to do is add the necessary components to the parent and pass the `counter` prop. The state is mutated *only* in the parent and then fed to the children.

Now we arrive at the moment where we need to decide which component should handle the state change. In our simple code example, the answer is obvious: we have only one parent. In the real world, this question may be much more difficult to answer. Luckily for us, we will look at state management strategies throughout this entire book. I hope, after reading this book, that you will be well equipped to choose the best place to store and manage your application state in your React Native app.

In the previous section, we went over high-level aspects of writing code in ReactJS. It's good to keep in mind the patterns we looked at, as they are just as useful in React Native development. And since we're familiar with ReactJS, we are ready to dive into the world of native apps written in JavaScript.

Understanding cross-platform software development

Before talking about React Native, we need to go over the landscape of mobile app development.

It is quite obvious that mobile apps can be created using native platform programming languages. The ones considered most modern are Swift, for iOS development, and Kotlin, for Android development. Many developers still use Objective-C and Java, respectively. However, when the market of mobile phones settled down with the two giants, Apple and Google, it was tempting to create solutions that could be written once for both platforms. Similarly, for websites, which can be opened in any browser, why can't we have apps that can be run on any device?

Looking for this mythical cross-platform solution was enticing to many companies. They were hiring separate teams from iOS and Android to end up with apps that do not look and feel the same.

The software development world is vast, and we can find many solutions to a single problem. Cross-platform development is not an exception to this rule. If you google `cross-platform apps`, you will find a solution from Microsoft, called **Xamarin**. You will also find **Flutter**, written in a language called **Dart**. And finally, you will find many solutions based on JavaScript. One of the first meaningful players was **Ionic**. Ionic is a framework, built in 2013, for development in AngularJS, and it uses **Apache Cordova** behind the scenes. Ionic developers build their apps using the exact same syntax they would use to create a website. At build time, a native app **wrapper** with a single WebView is created. The Ionic code is run inside this WebView. Given this structure, many people call Ionic apps **hybrid apps** to differentiate them from **cross-platform** apps.

React Native is a completely different solution. In its case, code is compiled into a complete native app. JavaScript code runs in the app and communicates with the phone's native modules through a **bridge**. But where did React Native come from, you may ask?

Let's dive into that topic in our next section.

Going over the history of React Native

Back in 2012, Facebook announced they were becoming a *mobile-first company*. Facebook realized its users spend more time on their phones than on computers. They needed to have their websites and apps working seamlessly on smart devices. However, the majority of Facebook engineers were web developers. The company started researching options to reuse the knowledge of those web developers for mobile development. After trying out a few different ideas, they didn't want to follow in the footsteps of Ionic, enclosing the apps inside WebViews. They needed something new.

That is when a developer named *Christopher Chedeau* made his mark on the history of software development. He teamed up with *Jordan Walke*, *Ashwin Bharambe*, and *Lin He* for an internal Facebook hackathon. Basing their work on the first attempts done by Jordan – who, by this time, had been able to generate *UILabel* in iOS from JavaScript – they created a working prototype that could generate native UI elements from JavaScript on the user device. And it took them only 2 days!

> **The history of React Native: Facebook's Open Source App Development Framework**
> You can read the article here: `https://www.techaheadcorp.com/blog/history-of-react-native/`.

After this initial success, Jordan and Christopher were able to continue working on their new product, named React Native, with an entire team of engineers.

After 3 years, they were ready to present what they had to the world. The official announcement for React Native took place at ReactJS Conf in 2015. This was the first ReactJS Conf, and React Native was presented during the keynote! That's how much faith Facebook had in this framework. I encourage you to check out the talk; you can find a link in the official ReactJS docs at `https://reactjs. org/blog/2015/02/18/react-conf-roundup-2015.html`.

Since 2015, React Native has grown and changed a lot. Some changes, such as the introduction of hooks and context, were simple follow-ups to changes happening in ReactJS. In other cases, changes were motivated by the community or proposed by the maintainers of the framework. React Native on `github.com` has a whole section called *Discussions and Proposals* (`https://github.com/ react-native-community/discussions-and-proposals`). Everyone is welcome to add anything they would like to discuss on the topic of React Native implementations, ecosystems, and so on. This board is a great resource for what is currently going on and what may be expected to happen in the future. One of the first issues on this board, the sixth issue to be exact, was a proposition for a *Lean Core*. By this time, React Native has been in the wild for at least 3 years and it has grown a lot. The framework has included implementations of UI details such as Switch, or native functionalities such as push notifications. One of the core maintainers of the repo proposed that all code that is not absolutely necessary be removed from the main package. You can read more details on *Lean Core* here: `https://github.com/react-native-community/discussions-and- proposals/issues/6`.

Of course, answering the question of "what is necessary" and "what isn't" is not easy. The *Lean Core* took a few months of discussions and breaking changes. The shape of the main React Native package today represents the results of this effort.

In the meantime, the *Lean Core initiative* energized the community to go ahead and create their own libraries, which could be useful for React Native apps. As of writing this book, there are hundreds of libraries to choose from when you decide to create a React Native app. There are UI libraries, navigation libraries, async storage management libraries, and many more. This is a blessing and a curse because not every library is well-written and maintained correctly. You can, unfortunately, happen to use something that may break your app in the future. So before running to your terminal and typing `yarn add`, you may want to use the React Native directory: `https://reactnative.directory`. This website provides metrics on open source libraries, which are very helpful when you want to add a good dependency to your project.

There are a few libraries that stand out so much, and they are considered to be *recommended* for React Native projects. Those libraries are usually pretty mature and well-maintained. One example is **React Navigation**, the go-to library for apps that need anything more than one screen. **React Native Testing Library** is a library officially coupled with Kent C. Dodd's **React Testing Library**. **Reanimated** is an animation library, which achieves better performance than any of its competitors.

An important part of the React Native ecosystem is **Expo**: `https://expo.dev/`. Expo is both a framework and a platform for React Native applications. It offers its users a set of tools useful for developing, building, and deploying apps.

What does that mean specifically? Expo is a thin layer on top of React Native, aimed at making the life of developers easier. If writing an app in React Native was like eating a grilled steak with your hands, Expo would be like eating Filet Mignon with a baked potato and a side of Caesar salad. In a fancy restaurant. You may very well prefer the former, but you cannot deny the obvious advantages of the latter. If you decide to use Expo, you will find local environment setup instructions in the official React Native docs: `https://reactnative.dev/docs/environment-setup`. Once the app is set up, you will be able to take advantage of the many components created and maintained by the Expo team. This way, you may save yourself a few headaches and performance problems. When you're ready to show your app to the world, you can upload your app bundle to the Expo website and use it for testing and deployment. As you can see, Expo is a very versatile tool.

Now that we're up to speed with the history and the current state of React Native, let's move on to looking at some real-world apps that use it.

Reviewing examples of popular apps using React Native

Now that we know a little bit about React Native, it's time to get excited about it. A great way to get excited about a new technology is to look at what that technology has already been used for. This is also a good strategy when you must decide to use a particular technology.

The obvious example comes from **Meta** – the birthplace of React Native. The very first implementations of ReactJS took place in Facebook Ads. It is fitting that React Native is used for that same feature on mobile devices. Facebook's mobile app is not entirely created with React Native, but some parts of it use it. That means the Facebook app is a React Native *brownfield* app. The opposite of that is apps written in React Native alone, and that sort of app is called *greenfield*.

While we're in the Metaverse, I will mention that the Instagram app uses React Native, as does the Oculus app.

Don't worry, Meta is not the only notable company using React Native. Discord not only uses React Native for their app, but they also write blog posts about how they maintain their app. In this Medium article, `https://blog.discord.com/how-discord-achieves-native-ios-performance-with-react-native-390c84dcd502`, the Discord team states that they adopted React Native as soon as it was open sourced, and they are still happy with their decision years later.

Shopify is another big player in the React Native ecosystem. They have an article on their blog entitled *React Native is the Future of Mobile at Shopify*: `https://shopify.engineering/react-native-future-mobile-shopify`. Shopify engineers also write more technical articles, for example, about accessibility: `https://www.shopify.com/partners/blog/react-native-accessibility`.

The website-builder giant **Wix** is also active in the React Native world. They have also written about their adventure with React Native (`https://medium.com/wix-engineering/react-native-at-wix-the-architecture-db6361764da6`) but they also create open source libraries, for example, this UI kit: `https://github.com/wix/react-native-ui-lib`.

Circling back to listing specific apps built with React Native, I have to mention **Coinbase**. Managing users' finances in a reliable manner is the top priority for this crypto market leader. They analyzed, iterated, and landed on using React Native as their main mobile technology. You can read their article about the transition from native technologies on their blog: `https://blog.coinbase.com/announcing-coinbases-successful-transition-to-react-native-af4c591df971`.

You may have heard of companies such as Tesla, Walmart, Salesforce, Bloomberg, and Vogue. You may have used apps such as Uber Eats, Artsy, Words with Friends, and SoundCloud Pulse. What do they have in common? Surprise! (Not really.) They all use React Native. You can find even more examples with links to articles in the React Native showcase: `https://reactnative.dev/showcase`.

Not all React Native stories are success stories, though. One famous case (by *famous*, I mean it was tweeted about for a few days) is Airbnb. Airbnb's website uses ReactJS, so it was logical for them to try React Native for their mobile app. After a few years of development, they hit development roadblocks and performance issues. Their app consists of a very big map that needs to work perfectly. The developers working on the app often needed help from React Native developers, which was a bottleneck for this web-technology-focused company. They announced their divorce from React Native in 2018: `https://medium.com/airbnb-engineering/sunsetting-react-native-1868ba28e30a`. Luckily, they still develop their amazing animation library, **Lottie** (`http://airbnb.io/lottie/#/`), which can be used in React Native apps.

Summary

Oof! That was a lot of theory for a programming book, right? However, even if you found it a little dry, I strongly believe this theoretical knowledge will be very useful for the next chapter. We have learned a little bit about the history of web development and about the motivations of the creators of both ReactJS and React Native. Knowing all of this will let us understand the ideas behind different state management solutions. In the next chapter, we will jump into the most basic way of managing state in a React Native app: with hooks and context.

2
Managing State in a Simple React App

In the previous chapter, we went over a brief history of web development, **JavaScript**, **ReactJS**, and **React Native**. Even though historical knowledge is not required to write great code, I find it useful. Once we learn why specific library creators encourage some patterns and discourage others, we can write code that is less error-prone and more performant. Ah yes! Writing code! That's why you're here, dear reader, isn't it? Well, I have good news. In this chapter, we will dive into code examples. We will start by looking at the most basic data and state management strategies in React: using state and props. We will then dive into a comparison of stateful and stateless components. Once we have a good understanding of how state works in React applications, we will move on to talking about hooks. We will finish off this chapter by completing a setup and configuration of our own little app.

Here are the bullet points of what we will cover:

- What is state and how is it different from props?
- What are stateful and stateless components?
- What are hooks and why use them?
- Setting up the example app

By the end of this chapter, you should feel comfortable with React code. We will also set up the base for our application. Even though applications can be very different from one another, this basic setup will remain the same for most of them. Feel free to reuse it for any other project you may want to work on.

Technical requirements

If you are familiar with **ReactJS** but you have not worked with **React Native** yet, you will be able to follow along with this section without any problem.

If you have never read or written any **ReactJS** or **React Native** code, it's important that you learn the basic concepts. Please head over to the official **React Native** documentation at `https://reactnative.dev/docs/intro-react` and familiarize yourself with key concepts such as **components, JSX, state, and props**.

A minimum requirement for this chapter is knowledge of Git, basic knowledge of **command-line interfaces** (**CLIs**), and a working knowledge of JavaScript.

What is state and how is it different from props?

Every **React Native** application is created to display some sort of data. It can be weather data, images, market data, maps… Using **React Native**, we manage how this data is displayed on our users' screens. **React Native** offers robust tools for styling and animating content. However, in this book, we are concentrating on the raw material of data used in your app.

In order to have a dynamic piece of data, existing **automagically** in sync with our component, we need to declare the list as a component state.

> **Important note**
> The most important thing to remember about state is this: state is managed within the component; it is the component **memory**.

Any changes in state will cause your component and all its children to re-render. This is an expected behavior: if your data changes, you want your UI to change as well. However, multiple component re-renders may cause your app to encounter performance issues.

Let's look at an example to better understand state. We will start off with a very basic component, containing a `<Text>` element and a `<Pressable>` element. `<Pressable>` is the recommended component to use in React Native applications in places where a web developer would use a `<button>` tag:

```
import React from "react";
import { View, Text, Pressable } from "react-native";

export const ManagedButton = () => {
  return (
    <View>
        <Text>this text will display the current status</Text>
        <Pressable onPress="">
            <Text>Press here to check/uncheck</Text>
        </Pressable>
    </View>
```

```
    );
};
```

As you can probably observe, dear reader, nothing will happen when the `<Pressable>` component is tapped because we haven't provided an `onPress` function.

We will now add state to this simple component. We will set a checked/unchecked text inside the `<Text>` component, linked to the component state:

```
import React, { useState } from "react";
import { View, Text, Pressable } from "react-native";

export const ManagedButton = () => {
    const [checkedState, setCHeckedState] =
      useState("unchecked");
  return (
    <View>
        <Text>this text will display the current status,
          which is: {checkedState}</Text>
      <Pressable onPress="">
          <Text>Press here to check/uncheck</Text>
      </Pressable>
    </View>
  );
};
```

Testing React Native code is a little more complicated than testing code made to run in browsers (as with JavaScript or ReactJS). Lucky for us, the good people at Expo created an online tool for testing code snippets. It's called Expo Snack and you can use it to test the preceding code at `https://snack.expo.dev/@p-syche/simplifying-state-management---chapter-2-example-1`.

Let's walk through the changes one by one. We start by adding an import of the `useState` hook from the React library on the first line. Then, inside the component, we set this variable:

```
const [checkedState, setCheckedState] = useState("unchecked");
```

The `useState` hook accepts an array, where the first item is the state value, and the second item is the function that will set the value. If you will not change the state in your component, you can omit the second argument. There is no official rule as per the names of the items in the array, but it is an accepted convention to name the setter function similarly to the state value, but with the `"set"` keyword. Last but not least, the `"unchecked"` string is passed to the `useState` hook. This is the default value of the `useState` hook. If you do not wish to set a default state, you may leave the parentheses empty.

Now that we have the state hook imported and the component state set with the `useState` hook, we can use it in our component. Hence, this line:

```
<Text>this text will display the current status, which is:
{checkedState}</Text>
```

The curly braces surrounding the state are part of **JSX**. **JSX** is a syntax extension to **JavaScript**, and it's the syntax used to write all **React** components. *"What does that mean in regular English?"* you ask, dear reader. It means that when writing in **JSX**, you can write any **JavaScript** code, plus you can write additional stuff, such as **component state** wrapped in curly braces. You could look at **JSX** compared to **JavaScript** as if it were a pirate speaking as compared to plain English. All English pirates will understand all English phrases, but a regular Englishman will not understand all pirate phrases. All right, matey? Let's move on then, yo ho ho!

We have the state set up, but our `<Pressable>` component still doesn't do anything, does it? Let's add an `onPress` function, which will set the state. The simplest way to achieve this is to pass the `setCheckedState` function from the `useState` hook right into the `onPress` function:

```
<Pressable onPress={setCheckedState("checked")}>
```

Now, when the `<Pressable>` button is pressed, it will change the state of the component, which in turn will change the text displayed in the `<Text>` component.

There is much more you can achieve with the `useState` hook. You can set it to any value you like, including an object. Every component can have multiple pieces of state, as many as you'd like, actually! If you would like to look at other examples of how state can be implemented in a React component, I invite you to check the first link from the *Further reading* section.

Let's move on to the second hero of this section: props. Props is a short name for **properties**. Props are **JavaScript** objects just like state; the biggest difference between them is that props are read-only.

> **Important note**
> The most important thing to remember about props is this: props are immutable (or read-only).

A natural flow of a **ReactJS** or **React Native** app is to have a parent component with some state—in our previous code example, it was the `"checked"`/`"unchecked"` state. The parent component has children: components with images or text, and so on, to whom we pass the state in the form of a prop. The children can **read** the state: whether the text should be `"checked"` or `"unchecked"`, in this case. But the children will never **change** the state of the text. The **state** of the text can only be changed within the parent component where state was declared. Let's update our code example to include a parent and a child component, with state set in the parent and passed to the child through props:

```
import React, { useState } from "react";
import { View, Text, Pressable } from "react-native";

const ManagedText = ({checkedState}) => {
  return (
      <Text>this text will display the current status,
        which is: {checkedState}</Text>
  );
};


export const ParentComponent = () => {
      const [checkedState, setCheckedState] =
        useState("unchecked");
    return (
        <View>
            <ManagedText checkedState={checkedState} />
              <Pressable onPress={() =>
                setCheckedState("checked")}>
              <Text>Press here to check/uncheck</Text>
            </Pressable>
        </View>
    );
  };
```

You can find the preceding code in this Expo Snack: `https://snack.expo.dev/@p-syche/ simplifying-state-management---chapter-2-example-2`.

Let's start with what remained the same as in the previous example. We have our <ParentComponent>, which, OK, was named <ManagedButton> before. But let's be honest, this component didn't change much from the previous version. The only change here is that instead of a <Text> component, we see a <ManagedText> component, with a mysterious checkedState property. This property is passed to the <ManagedText> component and then to the <Text> component inside it. Pressing the <Pressable> component will change the state of <ParentComponent>, which will also be reflected in the child component: <ManagedText>. I believe, dear reader, that the parent/child nomenclature is quite understandable and doesn't need additional explanations. As per the checkedState property, or prop for short, you should know that you can name it whatever you would like; there is no need to set the name of the prop to be the same as its value. You could write something like this, for example:

```
const ManagedText = (fancyComponentStuff) => {
  return (
      <Text>this text will display the current status,
        which is:{fancyComponentStuff}</Text>
  );
};


export const ParentComponent = () => {
      const [checkedState, setCheckedState] =
        useState("unchecked");
    return (
        <View>
            <ManagedText fancyComponentStuff={checkedState} />
            <Pressable onPress={setCheckedState("checked")}>
              <Text>Press here to check/uncheck</Text>
            </Pressable>
        </View>
    );
  };
```

If you're curious to learn more about props and state, you can head over to articles recommended by the official React team. They are listed in the *Further reading* section.

Now that you know what state and props are and how they are different from each other, in the following section, we will look at stateful and stateless components.

What are stateful and stateless components?

Whether you're completely new to the **React** world, or you've been here for a little while, you have probably heard the terms **stateful** and **stateless** components. These terms were especially useful before the introduction of hooks in **ReactJS** v16.8. Don't worry about hooks right now—we'll get to them toward the end of this chapter.

From a high-level perspective, **ReactJS** and **React Native** components are nothing more than **JavaScript** functions. The **React** library adds some specific features to those functions. One of those features is **state**, a special kind of component memory that we looked at in the previous section.

A React component that can accept state may look like this:

```
class Welcome extends React.Component {
  constructor(props) {
    super(props);
    this.state = {name: "World"}
  };
  render() {
    return <Text>Hello, {this.state.name}</Text>;
  }
}
```

This type of component is also commonly called a "class component" because of the way it needs to be declared. Class components, or stateful components, were first-class citizens until **ReactJS** v16.8. Any developer who needed to do anything with state would use this type of component. Unfortunately, these types of components had many downsides. They used **"lifecycle methods"**— special functions with very specific names, created to be run in a predetermined sequence. There are `componentDidMount()`, `componentWillUnmount()`, `shouldComponentUpdate()`, and a few others. These functions were a lifesaver for many developers facing edge cases. For example, they needed some data to be loaded before the rest of the **component**, or maybe they needed to make sure to clean up some side effect functions before the **component** unmounted. Unfortunately, this also meant that their **components** became increasingly complex logically. Trying to understand the flow of the code in a file containing multiple **"lifecycle methods"** is a real challenge. If you would like to learn more about lifecycle methods, please look at the *Further reading* section, where you will find a link to an article in the ReactJS documentation entitled *Adding Lifecycle Methods to a Class*.

Stateful components are also more difficult to test than **stateless components**, plus they compile slower and are bigger after compilation.

Stateless components, also known as **functional components**, are the lightweight brothers of class components. Here's an example of a stateless component:

```
const Welcome = (props) => {
  return <Text>Hello, World! </Text>;
}
```

Comparing the two example **components** shown in the preceding snippet, you should notice a big difference in the number of lines of code needed to write the given **component**. Our simple stateful **component** needed nine lines for what the **functional component** achieved in three!

This means **stateless components** are easier to write from a developer's point of view. They also don't need magical objects such as `constructor` or special **lifecycle methods** such as `componentDidUpdate`. They do, of course, have the great downside of not being able to manage state. So, an ideal **ReactJS** or **React Native** app would include at least one parent, a stateful component, which then would pass props to all kinds of stateless children components. However, there are hardly any ideal apps in the real world. Developers would very often write stateful components and add lifecycle methods to manage when UI updates should and should not happen.

This trend changed with the aforementioned **ReactJS** v16.8 when the concept of hooks was introduced in the **ReactJS** world, which we are going to look at in the next section.

What are hooks and why use them?

As I mentioned before, stateless components are generally easier to write and test. They should be the go-to component of **ReactJS** developers, but they were often overlooked because they could not manage state. At the beginning of 2019, the ReactJS team added **hooks** to the library. Hooks add state functionality to stateless components (therefore, it is better to only use the term **functional components**). One specific hook called `useState` is a function that returns a stateful value and a function to update it. You may recognize it from our previous section about state in React components.

Let's go back to our example of a stateful component, change it to a functional one, and add the `useState` hook, as follows:

```
import React, {useState} from "react";
import {Text} from "react-native";

const Welcome = () => {
  const [name, setName] = useState('World!');
  return <Text>Hello, {name}</Text>;
}
```

Ta-da! It looks so much cleaner than the previous example! We still have a component capable of holding and managing state changes, but it's much shorter than the stateful class component. I also feel this type of component has a very nice logical flow, where we declare the state value and the state setter function on one line.

If you want to see this code in action, you can go to `https://snack.expo.dev/@p-syche/` `example-of-functional-component-with-usestate`.

This is an **Expo Snack**—an equivalent of code snippets for web development.

Which hooks should you know?

The first hook we spoke about was `useState`, and that one is the absolute first you should familiarize yourself with. The second most used hook is `useEffect`. I also believe this is one of the best-named hooks. You can use it to add all sorts of side effects to your components. *"What is a side effect?"* you may ask, my dear reader. Let's try to grasp this concept using examples: imagine a social media app (much like the app we will be building in this book!). Now, let's imagine you are tasked with adding a likes counter. You have your parent **component** holding the likes button, and a `<Text>` **component** with a counter. It would look something like this:

```
const LikesParentComponent = () => {
    const getCounterNumberFromApi =
      someFunctionRetrievingDataFromAPI();
    const [counterNumber, setCounterNumber] =
      useState(getCounterNumberFromApi)
  return (
    <LikesComponent counterNumber={counterNumber} />
  );
};


const LikesComponent = (counterNumber) => {
    const [likeState, setLikedState] = useState
      ("haven't yet liked");
    return (
        <View>
            <Text>you {likeState} this post</Text>
            <Pressable onPress={setLikedState("liked")}>
              <Text>Press here to check/uncheck</Text>
            </Pressable>
              <Text>{counterNumber} other people liked this
                post</Text>
```

```
        </View>
    );
};
```

We are passing `counterNumber` from `<LikesParentComponent>` as a prop. Let's assume this parent component handles retrieving the number of likes from an API using the very nicely named `someFunctionRetrievingDataFromAPI()` function.

This is looking pretty good so far, right? We load our components; they retrieve the likes data from an API and pass it to our `<LikesComponent>`, which displays it nicely. But wait! What happens if the user touches the `<Pressable>` component? We will set `<Text>` to `liked`, but the counter will not go up! We simply cannot leave it like this! This is a classic side effect: a user action requires additional changes in component state. First of all, we cannot change `counterNumber` from within `<LikesComponent>` because, as we learned in the previous section on state and props, props are immutable. What can we do, then? We can use the state setter function from the parent component. This function can be passed as a prop. This means `<LikesParentComponent>` will invoke its child, like this:

```
<LikesComponent counterNumber={counterNumber}
setCounterNumber={setCounterNumber} />
```

So far, so good. Now, all we need to do is call this setter function at an appropriate time, which means when the button is pressed in `<LikesComponent>`. This is what it would look like using the `useEffect` hook:

```
const LikesComponent = (counterNumber, setCountNumber) => {
    const [likeState, setLikedState] = useState
      ("haven't yet liked");

    useEffect(() => {
        if (likeState === "liked") {
            setCounterNumber(counterNumber++)
        }
        else {
            setCounterNumber(counterNumber-1)
        }
    }, [likeState])

    return (
        <View>
            <Text>you {likeState} this post</Text>
```

```
          <Pressable onPress={setLikedState("liked")}>
            <Text>Press here to check/uncheck</Text>
          </Pressable>
            <Text>{counterNumber} other people liked this
              post</Text>
      </View>
    );
  };
```

As you may notice, the useEffect hook looks very different from the useState hook. Don't worry too much about this. These two hooks are the most used, and you will get used to the way they are conceived and consumed.

The inside of our example useEffect hook is a common if/else statement checking whether the value of the state equals "liked" or not. The most crucial and interesting part of this hook is the array at the very end. This array is called a dependency array. It is used to inform the hook function when it should run. In our case, the useEffect hook should run when the value of likeState changes.

The useEffect hook can be used to update different pieces of the app, to help with data fetching, for user-driven interactions, and so on. This hook is very powerful, but it has a very big risk: it can cause many re-renders when written incorrectly.

> **The most important thing to remember about useEffect**
> Make sure the dependency array of useEffect is correct!

As you may find in the official **ReactJS** documentation, the default behavior for effects is to fire the effect after **every** completed render. This may often be overkill. In such cases, we can pass an argument to useEffect's dependency array. If we set that, our effect will run *only* if any items in the dependency array change.

There are a few other built-in hooks. You don't have to know them all when starting to write **React Native** code. The two basic hooks—useState and useEffect—will be enough to get you started. When you get to a point where those two hooks are not enough, you can go back to the **ReactJS** documentation and read about other hooks. You can also write your own custom hooks useful for your particular app.

Now that we know what hooks are and why we use them, let's get started with setting up our sample app!

Setting up the example app

Ah! The moment you've probably been waiting for: actually creating an app!

We will start by preparing our development environment. You will need an **integrated development environment (IDE)** such as VS Code, Sublime Text, Atom, or anything else you may prefer. An IDE is all you need to write **React Native** code. But we also need a way to see what the code renders, don't we?

In the case of web development, we would simply use the browser to see and test our code. However, **React Native** apps cannot be easily tested in a web browser. They can and should be tested on real or simulated devices. In an ideal situation, you would have access to multiple phones, which you would plug into your computer via a USB in order to see your app. Most of us don't have multiple phones, though. That's why we can use phone simulators. There are two major players in the mobile world: Android and Apple. Android simulators are available for virtually any desktop platform thanks to the Android Studio app. Unfortunately, iPhone simulators can be run exclusively on Mac computers.

Setting up simulators can be a daunting task, but don't worry too much! There's **Expo**!

I spoke about **Expo** in the first chapter. If you skipped that part, let me give you a quick rundown: **Expo** is **React Native** development tooling. It makes building, testing, and publishing apps much easier. **Expo** is a wrapper on top of **React Native**, aimed at making the developer experience smoother.

Environment setup

Let's make sure your development environment is ready. As listed on the Expo website, you will need the latest Node, Git, and Watchman. Links to all of these can be found in Expo's documentation at `https://docs.expo.dev/get-started/installation/`. We will be using Yarn during development, so please make sure you have it installed. You can find detailed instructions here: `https://classic.yarnpkg.com/en/docs/install`. Once you have gone through the links, follow these steps:

1. When you're ready, go ahead and install Expo's CLI tools:

    ```
    $ npm install -global expo-cli
    ```

2. Verify that the installation was successful by running `expo whoami`. You're not logged in yet, so you will see **Not logged in**. You do not need an account to use Expo. If you want, you can create an account by running `expo register`, or you can log in to an existing account with `expo login`.

3. The next step is to install the Expo Go app on your phone. You can find it in the Android Store at `https://play.google.com/store/apps/details?id=host.exp.exponent` and on the App Store at `https://apps.apple.com/app/expo-go/id982107779`.

Thanks to Expo, it does not matter if you have a Mac computer or a Windows computer and what kind of phone you have. The **Expo Go** app will "automagically" work on Android and Apple devices.

4. We're all set—it's time to create the app. Go to your terminal and run the following command:

```
$ npx create-expo-app funbook-app
```

5. When prompted about templates, please choose **blank**.

    You can choose any name you like for your app. I suggested using "Funbook" because it sounds a little like "Facebook" and we'll be creating a social media app clone. Sticking with the same name as me will probably make it easier to follow along with code examples.

6. After app initialization is successfully run, you can go to your app's folder by running the following command:

```
$ cd funbook-app
```

7. And run the development server, like so:

```
$ expo start
```

    Or, if you're using Yarn, run this command:

```
$ yarn start
```

Expo CLI starts Metro Bundler, which is an HTTP server that compiles the JavaScript code of our app. You should see a QR code that you can now scan using the Expo Go app on your phone. You can run your Funbook app on as many devices as you'd like.

App development can seem a little daunting at first, but don't worry if not everything works perfectly on the first try. There's a big chance you will find the culprit in your terminal window. The terminal output is the best source of information for you.

If you see any errors in the terminal, or you feel a little bit lost, make sure to check the Expo installation documentation: https://docs.expo.dev/get-started/create-a-new-app/.

I set up a public repository that we will use throughout this book. You can find it here: https://github.com/PacktPublishing/Simplifying-State-Management-in-React-Native.

On the main branch of this repository, you will find an app that is already set up. Feel free to clone or fork this repository. Remember that if you want to run this app on your computer, you will still need to install **Expo** tools and other required libraries (node, watchman, and yarn).

App structure

Let us consider which surfaces and components we will need for a simplistic social media app. By "surface," I mean what would be in web development a "page." That is a big building block of the app, composed of many components, presented together on the screen.

Our app will definitely need a login surface, a social media feed surface, and a personal profile surface. We will also add a screen containing favorited posts and another one where the user can add their post. We will use fake data for the feed and profile, and a single username and password for logging in. We won't be implementing a registration flow in order to stay on the simple side of things.

We want to concentrate on data flows, so we will use a free social media UI kit to get the design "out of the way," so to speak. Here's a link to the design file we will use: `https://www.pixeltrue.com/free-ui-kits/social-media-app`.

App root

Our app will consist of at least five surfaces, which means we need to set up navigation to be able to move between those surfaces. The user will start off on the login surface. They will fill in their information and they will be redirected to the social media feed surface.

Obviously, we need a way for our users to move around the app. One of the most used navigation libraries is called **React Navigation**. This is a library created especially for **React Native** applications. It provides three types of navigation out of the box: Drawer navigation, Tab navigation, and Stack navigation. Drawer navigation is when you have a little drawer on the side of your app with links to different places in your app. Tab navigation will display tabs (either bottom or top) with links to different places. Stack navigation works like a stack of cards—each screen is a card having the ability to redirect to any other card. If you would like to know more about this library, you can find a link to the documentation in the *Further reading* section.

There are other navigation libraries out there, but React Navigation is by far the most popular one in the **React Native** community. It is also actively maintained and updated to work with the newest **React Native** versions.

We need to start by adding the library as a dependency to our project. To do that, follow these steps:

1. We can add the library by running the following command:

    ```
    $ yarn add @react-navigation/native
    ```

2. If you visit the documentation website, you will notice there are different CLI commands for "**Expo** managed projects" and "bare **React Native** projects." Make sure to follow the instructions for Expo-managed projects. In our case, we need to run the following command:

    ```
    $ expo install react-native-screens react-native-safe-area-context
    ```

3. We will need to display a login surface first, which will redirect our users to the main app screen. In order to do that, we will use a Stack navigator. Let's add its dependencies to our project, as listed here at `https://reactnavigation.org/docs/stack-navigator/`:

```
$ yarn add @react-navigation/stack
$ expo install react-native-gesture-handler
```

The last setup step for the stack navigator is importing the gesture handler library at the very top of our `App.js` file.

The stack navigator will be very useful to manage the login state of our app, but we will also need bottom tab navigation to move between the other screens once the user is logged in. Tab navigation feels very natural for app users. It is visible on all screens and makes using the app easy.

As for now, we will only need to run one command:

```
$ yarn add @react-navigation/bottom-tabs
```

This command adds bottom tab navigation as a dependency to our project so that we will be able to use it later.

You may wonder why we needed to add so many different dependencies separately. This is caused by how the **React Navigation** authors decided to structure their library. They were certain most people will not need every kind of navigation in their **app**, so why should they include it in their app bundle? Every library user can decide which part of **React Navigation** will be useful to them and include only that part.

Let's move on to adding a little bit of structure to our basic app. Every app is built with at least a couple of different surfaces, which in turn are built with components. Our basic social media clone app will need a login surface and a main surface, visible after login. Since we're creating a social media app, we will go ahead and call the main surface "**Feed**", since it will house the user's newsfeed. As we progress, we will surely add more surfaces, but those two will be a good starting point.

Setting up surfaces

The login surface will need an input field for the username, an input field for the password, and a button to log in. But for now, we will create a dummy component with some text.

We will start by creating the login surface. You may wonder what it means to "create a surface." What I mean by it is that some of the components will be wrappers for entire surfaces of the app. Some people prefer to call them screens, and in web development, you would call them sites or pages. From a coding standpoint, they are components just like any other component. But we decide that, logically, they represent a bigger piece of the app, and we put them in a special folder, called `surfaces`.

Here's our login surface:

```
// ./src/surfaces/Login.js
import React from "react";
import { View, Text } from "react-native";

export const Login = () => {
  return (
    <View>
      <Text>this will be the login screen</Text>
    </View>
  );
};
```

As you may notice it is, in fact, a dummy component, named Login, and placed in the surfaces folder.

Using that same logic, we will create a Feed surface, which should be displayed after the users log in:

```
// ./src/surfaces/Feed.js

import React from "react";
import { View, Text } from "react-native";

export const Feed = () => {
  return (
    <View>
      <Text>this will be the feed screen</Text>
    </View>
  );
};
```

We have the two basic pieces of the app ready; now we need to put them together. This is where React Navigation comes into play.

Every React Native app needs a root file, just as every website needs an index.html file at the root. This root file is usually called App.js. This is the **source of truth** (**SOT**) for displaying anything and everything. You can think of it as a trunk of a tree, with many branches sprouting from it. The branches are different app surfaces in this metaphor. You got that, right? I'm sure you did! You're smart! After all, you *are reading my* book.

Let's set up the parent component to display the correct flow—first, the login screen, and then, the feed:

```js
// ./App.js
import 'react-native-gesture-handler';
import React, { useState } from "react";
import { NavigationContainer } from "@react-navigation/native";
import { createStackNavigator } from "@react-navigation/stack";
import { createBottomTabNavigator } from "@react-navigation/
  bottom-tabs";
import { Login } from "./src/surfaces/Login";
import { Feed } from "./src/surfaces/Feed";

const Stack = createStackNavigator();
const Tab = createBottomTabNavigator();

function Home() {
  return (
    <Tab.Navigator>
      <Tab.Screen name="Feed" component={Feed} />
    </Tab.Navigator>
  );
}

export default function App() {
  const [userLoggedIn, setIsUserLoggedIn] = useState(true);
  return (
    <NavigationContainer>
      <Stack.Navigator>
        {!userLoggedIn ? (
          <Stack.Screen name="Login" component={Login} />
        ) : (
          <Stack.Screen
            name="Home"
            component={Home}
            options={{ headerShown: false }}
          />
        )}
```

```
        </Stack.Navigator>
      </NavigationContainer>
  );
}
```

You can find the preceding code in this Expo Snack: `https://snack.expo.dev/@p-syche/ simplifying-state-management---chapter-2-example-3`.

In the preceding code, you will notice we used the `useState` hook. This way, we easily added state to our functional `App` component. We set up our initial state to be `false`—users opening the app for the first time are not supposed to be logged in. When the user logs in, they are redirected to the second "card" in our stack. This "card" is the `Home` component. This is a wrapper component used to hold the bigger part of our app: all other surfaces besides `Login` with tabbed bottom navigation. As you may notice, the navigators are nested: tabbed navigation is inside the stack navigator. This is a common and useful practice in **React Native** apps. You can read more about nesting navigators in the **React Navigation** documentation here: `https://reactnavigation.org/docs/ nesting-navigators`.

And there we go! We have set up an app using **Expo**. We added multiple components representing the future surfaces of the app. We also added and configured the **React Navigation** library. Our app is not very pretty right now, but it should work. You can see it on your phone through the Expo Go app, or in phone simulators on your computer screen.

I set up a public repository on GitHub so that you, dear reader, can more easily follow along with the code snippets and examples presented in this book. You can find the repo here: `https://github. com/PacktPublishing/Simplifying-State-Management-in-React-Native`. Feel free to clone or fork it. The `main` branch includes the basic app setup. Every state management library implementation is on a different branch. We will discuss the details as we move forward. If you decide to use this repository, you will notice the styles from the UI kit are implemented. We will not focus on styling in this book, but it is a nice addition to any app.

Summary

We have done some really good work here! We started out by looking at simple code examples necessary to understand some ReactJS coding concepts such as component state and props, lifecycle methods, and hooks. It is important to understand and internalize the differences between state and props, and stateful and stateless components. A good grasp of those concepts can determine whether your app will run smoothly or not.

After diving into important React concepts and examples, we moved on to actually setting up our app. This is a very exciting moment! We have our foundation, and we are ready to build a real-life social media clone app. In the next chapter, we will get comfortable previewing and debugging our app. We will set up all necessary surfaces, we will add example data, and finally, we will style the app. I can't wait!

Further reading

- React Native's documentation—example of components with state: `https://reactnative.dev/docs/intro-react#state`.

- State versus Props:

  `https://lucybain.com/blog/2016/react-state-vs-pros/`.

  `https://github.com/uberVU/react-guide/blob/master/props-vs-state.md`.

- Adding Lifecycle Methods to a Class—ReactJS docs:

  `https://reactjs.org/docs/state-and-lifecycle.html#adding-lifecycle-methods-to-a-class`.

- A full blogpost about hooks:

  `https://pl.reactjs.org/blog/2019/02/06/react-v16.8.0.html`.

- ReactJS documentation on hooks:

  `https://reactjs.org/docs/hooks-reference.html#useeffect`.

- React Navigation documentation:

  `https://reactnavigation.org/docs/getting-started/`.

- React Navigation—bottom tab navigation: `https://reactnavigation.org/docs/tab-based-navigation`.

- React Navigation guide on authentication flow: `https://reactnavigation.org/docs/auth-flow`.

- React Navigation guide on nesting navigators: `https://reactnavigation.org/docs/nesting-navigators`.

Part 2 – Creating a Real, Working App

In this part, we will concentrate on building a real, functioning mobile app. Readers will learn to plan out app features and configure the real setup of the Funbook app; then, they will learn how to style a React Native app so that it matches a given design, and how to pull in real data.

This part includes the following chapters:

- *Chapter 3, Planning and Setting Up the Funbook App*
- *Chapter 4, Styling and Populating the Funbook App*

3

Planning and Setting Up the Funbook App

In the previous chapter, we learned how to set up a React Native app. The steps we followed, installing dependencies and building and running the app, are common for most apps you may want to build. Now, it's time to focus on the specifics of the app we will be building in this book. We want to create a social media clone app so that we can compare different state management solutions in that app. In this chapter, we will plan and build our example app using only React Native built-in solutions – state, props, hooks, and context. We will take the following steps:

- Planning the needed surfaces and components
- Planning data flows in the app
- Getting comfortable previewing and debugging the app

By the end of this chapter, you will have a good idea of planning out development work for the Funbook app. You will also find out how to work comfortably with a React Native app.

Technical requirements

In order to follow along with this chapter, you will need some knowledge of JavaScript and ReactJS. If you have followed the first two chapters of this book, you should be able to go forward without any issues.

Feel free to use an IDE of your choice, as React Native does not need any specific functionality. Currently, the most popular IDEs for frontend developers are Microsoft's VSCode, Atom, Sublime Text, and WebStorm.

You may have followed the setup guide from the previous chapter. In case you didn't set up your own app, you can clone the repo dedicated to this book:

`https://github.com/PacktPublishing/Simplifying-State-Management-in-React-Native`.

In this repository, you will find a very basic app, as it was set up in the previous chapter. You will also find folders with chapter names. Not surprisingly, each folder holds a version of the Funbook app as described in a given chapter.

Planning the needed surfaces and components

As I've mentioned before, we can divide our app into surfaces, and then break down the surfaces into smaller, reusable components. Our app will need the following surfaces:

- **Login**
- **Feed** (which is also our **Home** surface)
- **Add Post**
- **Favorites**
- **Profile**

We have those surfaces set up as files in our project. Let's take a quick look at the free design file we'll be using for our app. You can find the file here: `https://www.pixeltrue.com/free-ui-kits/social-media-app`.

You can download this file and open it in Figma or import it at `https://www.figma.com`. If you don't have a Figma account yet – don't worry, they're free. You can take a moment right now to look at the actual file, or if a screenshot is enough for you, let's look together:

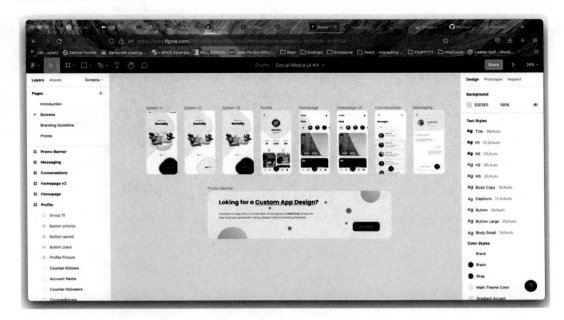

Figure 3.1 – Figma website with the design template

Let's zoom in on the home page:

Figure 3.2 – Design of the home surface

You may have noticed there are five items in the bottom tabs on the design. Which one are we missing? The chat bubble. Let's go ahead and add this surface to our app. I encourage you to add this file on your own and then come back here and check against my example. Here's what my `Conversations` surface looks like so far:

```
import React from "react";
import { View, Text } from "react-native";

export const Conversations = () => {
  return (
    <View>
      <Text>this will be the chat screen</Text>
    </View>
  );
};
```

And here's the `App.js` file with the newly added screen:

```
import "react-native-gesture-handler";
import React, { useState } from "react";
import { NavigationContainer } from "@react-navigation/native";
import { createStackNavigator } from "@react-navigation/stack";
import { createBottomTabNavigator } from "@react-navigation/
  bottom-tabs";
import { Login } from "./src/surfaces/Login";
import { Feed } from "./src/surfaces/Feed";
import { Profile } from "./src/surfaces/Profile";
import { Favorites } from "./src/surfaces/Favorites";
import { AddPost } from "./src/surfaces/AddPost";
import { Conversations } from "./src/surfaces/Conversations";

const Stack = createStackNavigator();
const Tab = createBottomTabNavigator();

function Home() {
  return (
    <Tab.Navigator>
      <Tab.Screen name='Feed' component={Feed} />
```

```
        <Tab.Screen name='Conversations'
          component={Conversations} />
      <Tab.Screen name='AddPost' component={AddPost} />
      <Tab.Screen name='Favorites' component={Favorites} />
      <Tab.Screen name='Profile' component={Profile} />
    </Tab.Navigator>
  );
}
[...]
```

Okay! Looking good so far!

Now that we have our main surfaces set up, let's try to analyze which elements are good candidates for reusable components.

Looking back at the design file, let's start with the **Home** surface. At the top, we see a horizontal list of avatars and a list of repetitive cards below. Each card has an author image, a title, a favorite count, and a conversation count. So, the home component should be built out of avatar and card components.

Moving on to the **Conversations** screen: it consists of a search bar and a list of cards with the name of the person in the conversation and the last message exchanged. When a message is clicked, we will go to the screen named **Messaging** in the Figma file, where we will see a bigger avatar, a list of messages, and an input box. Remember we already have avatars on the home page; let's see whether we can reuse an avatar component. Maybe only to some extent, since the styles are not the same for the home avatars, the conversations avatars, and the messaging avatars. They are all round images, but they have different borders and sizes. Maybe we could create an avatar component that accepts size and border style as a prop. That's a pretty good idea! We'll try to achieve this when we get to writing code.

The last detailed surface we will in our free design file is **Profile**. We have yet another avatar here; this one is not even round. It's followed by the username, some statistics, and a two-column list of pictures and bookmarks. Since we're not going to be implementing bookmarks, we will exchange the bookmarks from the design for favorites. You may notice that the two columns are built with two different styles of elements, and that's probably how we should also create our components: one component for cards in the images column and one component for the **Favorites** card column.

Last but not least: the bottom tab bar. Our design file includes four regular icons and one with a different style. Styling React Navigation components is a separate task altogether, as we will need to read the documentation to find out how to implement a custom icon, active and inactive styles, as well as custom styles.

Since we are using a free design file, it does not cover all the surfaces we want to create. I am very happy we have this free resource at our fingertips, and we'll try to use the general styles and components to figure out what the remaining two of our surfaces should look like.

The **Login** surface should surely consist of two inputs: the username and password. We will re-use the input visible on the **Messaging** screen in Figma, and the background of the splash screen. As for the surface needed for adding posts, we'll have a rounded square for the image –to match the **Home** surface – and an input for the title of the post.

Let's summarize our plan: we have all our surfaces created. We will proceed to create the components necessary for the surfaces. We will create an avatar component, that we will use on the **Home**, **Conversations**, and **Messaging** surfaces. We will create a card component for the **Home** surface. We will then create another card component for the **Conversations** surface, along with a search box component. We will need to hook up the navigation to move correctly from **Conversations** to **Messaging**. On the **Messaging** surface, we will reuse the avatar component, a component for displaying messages, and a reusable input component. Moving on to the **Profile** screen, we will create a profile avatar component, components for profile statistics and components for cards of images, and different components for cards of favorited items. We will then move on to composing the **Login** screen using input box components created previously for the messaging screen. We will finish by completing the **Add Post** surface, using a version of the **Home** surface card and input. I don't recommend creating all the files beforehand, as a lot of things may change while we create the actual components.

Before we start writing components let's try to analyze what data will be needed for our app.

Planning data flows in the app

This is a part of app development that usually does not fall under the responsibilities of the frontend developer. The clients will often determine what data they want, and that data is organized by the backend developers. However, if you can participate in the way the data flows are organized, you will make your future work easier. Given that we are only building the frontend of an app using example data, we are free to organize it however we like.

We will use the design file again, as the basis for what work needs to be done. Starting with the **Home** screen, we know we need a list of users and a list of items to be displayed on the **Home** surface. As per the **Conversations** surface, we will need a list of conversations with respective usernames and messages. We will also need data for each one of the conversations, so we can display it on the **Messaging** surface. On the **Profile** surface, we will need a list of data pertinent to the user (name, avatar image, statistics), and two lists of images: added images and liked images. As per the surfaces missing from the design, we will need a login and password for the **Login** screen. We will not need any sample data for the **Add Post** surface.

Working with real data makes it easier to visualize the future shape of the app and of specific components. That is why I set up GitHub pages of the book repository to hold our sample data. You can find them on GitHub Pages (`https://packtpublishing.github.io/Simplifying-State-Management-in-React-Native/`) or in the main book repository in the `docs/` folder: `https://github.com/PacktPublishing/Simplifying-State-Management-in-React-Native/tree/main/docs`.

> **Browsing through sample data**
>
> You can see the example data used in the app whenever you'd like. Check out the data branch of the main repository here: `https://github.com/PacktPublishing/Simplifying-State-Management-in-React-Native/blob/data/docs/index.md` and look in the `docs/` folder. You can copy anything you'd like to your own projects.

The biggest and most obvious piece of the data puzzle we will need is a list of users. You can view the file on GitHub here: `https://github.com/PacktPublishing/Simplifying-State-Management-in-React-Native/blob/main/docs/users.json`. Our app will consume the raw JSON file, which can be accessed through the following link: `https://raw.githubusercontent.com/PacktPublishing/Simplifying-State-Management-in-React-Native/main/docs/users.json`.

You may wonder why I added user IDs if we're building a simple app with example data. The reason is that we will use the user data for a list of avatars on the **Home** surface. We will create this list with React and React requires that every item in a list has a unique `key` prop. Theoretically, we could use the image URL as our unique key and then try to remember not to use the same picture for more than one person. However, using an ID is a much cleaner solution. It is also closer to what you would see in a real-world app.

Now that we have a user list, let's take a look at what a specific user profile might look like. Our user will need an ID, which should match the record with their name in the `users.json` file. They also have a name and avatar image URL. We need to know how many posts, followers, and users following the given user has. Finally, we need two lists of images: added and liked images. Take a look at the `john_doe.json` file – that's what our example user profile data looks like.

Moving on to the **Home** surface: we will use the same data as in the `users.json` file here to display the list of avatars, so we don't need to add any additional avatar list data here. It will be followed by a list of items to be displayed in the form of cards with images. The example data is available in the `home.json` file.

Let's create our sample dataset for the conversations. It's not very complicated; it includes a username, a user avatar URL, a message, and an ID. We will need the conversation ID to correctly display conversation details on the **Messaging** surface.

Finally, we should create sample data for the **Messaging** surface. We will create a separate folder for conversation data, called `messages`. Inside that folder, we will create a few files for conversations. Every file is named by the conversation ID, which should make data fetching easier and more readable.

As for the **Login** screen, we will use a very small JSON file, which will hold a username and password. We will use this data to create user flows when the **Login** form is filled out correctly or incorrectly.

Looking at the JSON files, you will notice some data is repeated in a few files; namely, the user ID, user's name, and avatar image URL. In a real-world app, this could cause issues in the future, where data updated in place of the app will not be properly updated or available somewhere else. That is why we will remove all references to user names and avatar images and leave only the user ID, which we will use to get the other data from the `users.json` file.

And there we have it! A big list of users that we will use in different parts of the app, data for the **Home** surface, the **Profile** surface, and **Conversations**. We're ready to create our components! Right? Right! However, we need to get comfortable previewing and debugging our app first.

Getting comfortable previewing and debugging the app

Have you been looking to see whether your code runs correctly on a device or a simulator? If not, let's see how you can see it. The first thing you need to do is run this command in your terminal:

```
$ yarn start
```

When `expo` is done setting up your development server, you can hit "*i*" for an iPhone simulator (if you're working on a Mac computer), "*a*" for an android simulator (if you have Android Studio installed), or you can take your phone and use the Expo Go app.

Whichever one you choose, you will see a browser window open automatically on your device. This browser window looks like this:

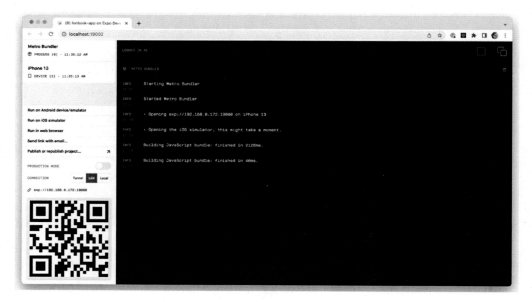

Figure 3.3 – Expo developer tools in the browser

If you want to see your app on your phone, you'll find the QR code to scan in the Expo Go app right here. You will see error messages here; you can even use this page to publish your app.

I like working with an iPhone simulator open. Here's what our app looks like set up on my computer:

Figure 3.4 – iPhone 13 with iOS 15.2 simulator screenshot

Hopefully, you see something similar. If you don't, you can always clone the GitHub repository, or compare your code to the one that's published. The state of the app you see in the preceding screenshot is what should be seen on the main branch of the repo located here: https://github.com/PacktPublishing/Simplifying-State-Management-in-React-Native.

Take some time to play around with the app. Try creating some obvious errors, such as writing plain text outside of the <Text /> component, maybe using a <div> tag, or not closing a tag.

We will practice code changes on our bottom tab navigation. We will not be creating any components for that.

Customizing the appearance of the tab navigator can be achieved by setting properties when the navigator is set up. We can also add some specific per-screen options. Our bottom tab navigator will use icons for tabs, so we will need to start by importing an icon library into the main App.js file. We will use a library called @expo/vector-icons. This library is installed by default on all projects initialized with expo.

> **Adding libraries**
>
> Before adding any additional dependencies and libraries, make sure to check the Expo documentation to see whether the library you want is not installed already. If you do need to add something, make sure to add libraries compatible with the Expo workflow.

Expo has done all the heavy lifting for us; we have a big icon library at our fingertips. All we need to do is use it to add icons to our navigator. We will start by adding simple icons to four of the five items:

```
import Ionicons from "@expo/vector-icons/Ionicons";


// …

function Home() {
  return (
    <Tab.Navigator
      screenOptions={({ route }) => ({
        tabBarIcon: ({ focused, color, size }) => {
          let iconName;

          if (route.name === "Feed") {
            iconName = focused ? "md-home" : "md-home-outline";
          } else if (route.name === "Conversations") {
            iconName = focused ? "chatbox" : "chatbox-outline";
          } else if (route.name === "Favorites") {
            iconName = focused ? "heart" : "heart-outline";
          } else if (route.name === "Profile") {
              iconName = focused ? "person-circle" :
                "person-circle-outline";
          }
```

```
        return <Ionicons name={iconName} size={size}
color={color} />;
      },
      tabBarActiveTintColor: "#25A0B0",
      tabBarInactiveTintColor: "#000000",
    })}
  >
    <Tab.Screen name='Feed' component={Feed} />
      <Tab.Screen name='Conversations'
        component={Conversations} />
    <Tab.Screen name='AddPost' component={AddPost} />
    <Tab.Screen name='Favorites' component={Favorites} />
    <Tab.Screen name='Profile' component={Profile} />
  </Tab.Navigator>
  );
}
```

We added a simple if statement to <Tab.Navigator>, where we give it specific instructions on what component should be displayed. Every time we're displaying a <Ionicons> component from the @expo/vector-icons library, however, we're feeding it different props. We'll leave the AddPost item for now. Once we create a reusable button component, we'll come back here and add it.

What we can customize further now is the tabBar label. As per the design, the label should not be displayed. We need to add another property to <Tab.Navigator>:

```
// ...
tabBarInactiveTintColor: "#000000",
tabBarShowLabel: false,
// ...
```

Looking good! Now, how about the header? Our app has a very generic header with a white background and the title of the given surface. As you can see on the design, some surfaces don't have titles (such as **Profile** or **Messaging**) and others have a title on a transparent background. React Navigation is responsible for the look of the header, so let's set it right now. We will add yet another prop to <Tab. Navigator>:

```
// ...
tabBarInactiveTintColor: "#000000",
tabBarShowLabel: false,
```

```
headerTransparent: true,
// ...
```

Yay! That worked – but wait, the text that was displayed on the screen is now behind a fixed, transparent header!

Figure 3.5 – iPhone simulator showing UI issues

We need to make sure the contents of our app won't ever fly off the screen like this. It's not an easy task to achieve, especially with so many screen shapes, notches, and digital buttons. Luckily for us, the creators of React Navigation added a wrapper component called `<SafeAreaView>`. We have to add the `SafeAreaProvider` component around `<NavigationContainer>`. This component uses React Context "under the hood." In order to use this context, we need to add `<SafeAreaView>` around each one of our surfaces. The main app component will look like this:

```
export default function App() {
  const [userLoggedIn, setIsUserLoggedIn] = useState(true);
  return (
    <SafeAreaProvider>
      <NavigationContainer>
```

```
      <Stack.Navigator>
       // ...
      </Stack.Navigator>
    </NavigationContainer>
  </SafeAreaProvider>
  );
}
```

Let's add `<SafeAreaView>` around the `<Feed>` component. Do you see any improvement over what we saw before? No? That's because there's one more gotcha: we need to add the `{{flex: 1}}` style to the wrapper component. Okay, the surface looks better – the text is contained on the screen – but it's still behind the header…

Figure 3.6 – Close-up of the iPhone simulator with changes to the UI

We want to add padding to the top of the surface so that our content will begin below the header. We want to determine the height of the header without having to hardcode any pixel values. **React Navigation** comes to the rescue again, by providing a custom hook called `useHeaderHeight()`. The Feed component looks like this now:

```
import React from "react";
import { SafeAreaView } from "react-native-safe-area-context";
import { View, Text } from "react-native";
import { useHeaderHeight } from "@react-navigation/elements";

export const Feed = () => {
  const headerHeight = useHeaderHeight();

  return (
      <SafeAreaView style={{ flex: 1, paddingTop: headerHeight
        }}>
      <View>
```

```
          <Text>this will be the feed screen</Text>
        </View>
    </SafeAreaView>
  );
};
```

And the app should look like this:

Figure 3.7 – iPhone simulator with fixed UI

Make sure to add `<SafeAreaView>` to all surfaces if you're following along with this book. If you prefer to see the code changes on GitHub, you will find them on the branch called `chapter-3`: `https://github.com/PacktPublishing/Simplifying-State-Management-in-React-Native/tree/main/chapter-3`.

If you're wondering why we're adding header styles to the `<Tab.Navigator>` and not the root component, I invite you to take a look at the `<Stack.Navigator>` we have set up at the root of our app, in preparation for a **Login** screen. In the `<Stack.Screen>` component, you will notice the following option:

```
options={{ headerShown: false }}
```

We are telling React Navigation to hide the header of `<Stack.Navigator>` and display the header of the nested `<Tab.Navigator>`. This nested `<Tab.Navigator>` is also the one we need to style. Go ahead and change the `headerShown` option in your project and observe what happens. You should see another header show up in the app with the Home title! That's because we've named Home the main parent component, used for creating `<Tab.Navigator>`. Make sure to change the `headerShown` option back to `false`, before getting back to work on our app.

I hope you're getting comfortable with making changes and previewing them in your app. Let's finish this section by adding a custom font. We'll use a library provided by Expo again: Expo Google Fonts. If you take a quick look at the design file, you'll find the name of the font used, it's a Google font called Poppins.

We'll go ahead and import the font into the `Feed` component, add it as a `style` prop to the `<Text>` component, and… oh no! Problem!

Figure 3.8 – iPhone simulator displaying an error

Even though this huge red box seems to be screaming at us, there's no need to worry. All we need to do is read the error. It states that `@expo-google-fonts/poppins` is not defined. Of course! We need to install this font in our project. Let's run the following commands in the terminal:

```
$ expo install expo-font
$ expo install @expo-google-fonts/poppins
```

The error should be gone. Now, we can safely add our font family to the `<Text>` component. Or can we?

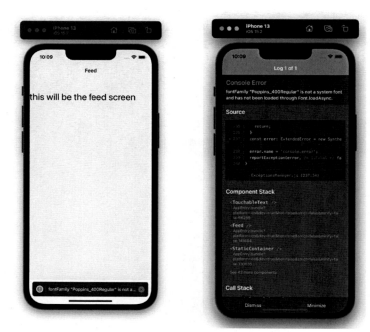

Figure 3.9 – iPhone simulators displaying an error toast message and details

The font has not been loaded... Let's go back to the Expo documentation and make sure we loaded everything correctly.

According to the documentation, we first need to use the `useFont` hook with an `AppLoading` wrapper around the root component! Here's what we need to add to the `App.js` file:

```
export default function App() {
  const [userLoggedIn, setIsUserLoggedIn] = useState(true);
  let [fontsLoaded] = useFonts({
    Poppins_400Regular,
```

```
  });

  if (!fontsLoaded) {
    return <AppLoading />;
  }
  return (
// ...
```

And there we have it. Now, the app works correctly, and we can add the `fontFamily` style wherever we'd like:

```
<Text style={{ fontFamily: "Poppins_400Regular"}}>
```

In this section, we got comfortable changing code, previewing our app, and handling errors. Now, we're ready to write and style components in the next chapter.

Summary

In this chapter, we planned our app and got comfortable previewing and debugging it. Both of these steps are vital to creating a good developer experience. First of all, we do not want to face any major surprises – that's why we want to plan ahead. You could compare this to how a building is built. No self-respecting construction worker would start setting up walls and doors before making, or at least looking at, a blueprint. We, as software developers, are building a digital product and not a building, but we're using the word "to build" for very good reasons.

Second of all, we need to know how to check whether what we're writing is actually working. Your code may look logical to you, but that does not mean that it will work after JavaScript tries to understand your logic. That is why every web developer has a browser window open while working, and why a mobile app developer needs to look at a phone or a phone simulator. Since we will be spending quite a lot of time looking at our apps on phones, it's good to get comfortable.

Now, dear reader, we are ready to continue our journey into the weeds of React Native! In the next chapter, we will build the components we planned above. We will also add styles to match our beautiful design. We will encounter a few classical problems of React Native and a few quirks – and we will have a nice-looking app at the end!

Further reading

- `https://docs.expo.dev/guides/icons/` – Expo icons guide.
- `https://reactjs.org/docs/context.html` – React context.
- `https://github.com/expo/google-fonts` – Expo Google Fonts.

4

Styling and Populating the Funbook App

In the previous chapter, we planned what surfaces and components will be needed for our app based on the design file. We also got comfortable previewing and debugging the app – at least I hope you got comfortable, my dear reader! Whether you're using an iPhone or Android simulator or a real device with the Expo Go app, make sure you prefer checking your app that way. There's no wrong answer for previewing apps built with Expo. In this chapter, we will style our surfaces and components. We will finally see an app that looks, hopefully, close to the design! After that, we will add some real data.

Here's a very short list of what we're planning to achieve in this chapter:

- Creating and styling components
- Pulling in data for the app

By the end of this chapter, we will have a good-looking app that fetches data from an external API. Feel free to follow closely or write your own code.

Technical requirements

In order to follow along with this chapter, you will need some knowledge of JavaScript and ReactJS. If you have followed along the first two chapters of this book, you should be able to go forward without any issues.

Feel free to use an IDE of your choice, as React Native does not need any specific functionality. Currently, the most popular IDEs for frontend developers are Microsoft's Visual Studio Code, Atom, Sublime Text, and WebStorm.

The code snippets provided in this chapter are here to illustrate what we should be doing with the code. They do not provide the whole picture. For a better experience of coding along, open the GitHub repo in your IDE and look at the files in there.

If you get stuck or lost, you can check the code in the GitHub repo: `https://github.com/PacktPublishing/Simplifying-State-Management-in-React-Native/tree/main/chapter-4`.

Creating and styling components

It's time to create some real components! Let's start with the home surface.

I like to work from top to bottom, so we will start with the header. Our free design template includes the app name ("Socially") and a bell icon at the top of the feed surface. We won't be implementing notifications in our example app, so we'll overlook this part of the design file. Adding styles to the header is done through React Navigation. We will add the following properties to `<Tab.Navigator>`:

```
// …
  headerTransparent: true,
  headerTitleAlign: "left",
  headerTitleStyle: {
  paddingTop: 140,
  paddingBottom: 40,
  textAlign: "left",
  fontWeight: "bold",
},
// …
```

As we analyzed the home surface before, we know we need to create two parts of this surface: a list of avatars and a list of cards with images. The list of avatars will use a horizontal `FlatList` component. The first item on the list is different; it's a button used by the user to add content. We'll add a `ListHeaderComponent` property to `FlatList`, where we will add this special item. Let's create a placeholder component for now:

```
// src/components/ListHeaderComponent
import React from "react";
import { View, Text } from "react-native";

export const ListHeaderComponent = () => {
  return (
    <View>
      <Text>List Header component placeholder</Text>
    </View>
```

```
  );
};
```

In the preceding code, we created a component named `ListHeaderComponent`, so we can import it into `FlatList`. So far, this component only displays placeholder text.

I added a few profile images exported from the design file into the `assets` folder. We'll use them for our list of avatars.

Here's what the `ListOfAvatars` component looks like:

```
// src/components/ListOfAvatars.js
import React from "react";
import { View, Text, FlatList} from "react-native";
import { ListHeaderComponent } from "./ListHeaderComponent";

const arrayOfAvatars = [
  {
    id: 1,
    url: "",
  },
  {
    id: 2,
    url: "",
  },
  {
    id: 3,
    url: "",
  },
];

export const ListOfAvatars = () => {
  const renderItem = ({ item }) => {
    return <Text>{item.id}</Text>
  };
  return (
    <View style={{ paddingTop: 30 }}>
      <FlatList
        data={arrayOfAvatars}
```

```
            renderItem={renderItem}
            keyExtractor={(item) => item.id}
            horizontal
            ListHeaderComponent={<ListHeaderComponent />}
        />
    </View>
  );
};
```

Remember to import the necessary components from **React Native** – in this case, we need to import `FlatList`. You may also notice I set up a very simple data array to be fed into the list of avatars. We'll manage connecting this component to our sample data later.

If you prefer to look at this code on your screen instead of the book, you can always look in the repo. The code we are working on currently can be found in the `chapter-3` branch: `https://github. com/PacktPublishing/Simplifying-State-Management-in-React-Native/ tree/main/chapter-3`.

Once we have `FlatList` set up with links to actual images, we can change the `<Text>` component for an `<Image>` component, feed it data from our array, add some styles so that the images are rounded, and we're done!

We'll add a list of cards, which will be very similar to the list of avatars. We'll also use an array with temporary data and add some styling, and we should end up with a component looking like this:

```
// src/components/ListOfCards.js

export const ListOfCards = () => {
  const renderItem = ({ item }) => {
    return (
      <Image
        style={{
          width: "100%",
          height: 288,
          borderRadius: 20,
          marginBottom: 32,
        }}
        source={{
          uri: item.url,
        }}
```

```
        />
      );
    };
    return (
      <View style={{ paddingVertical: 30 }}>
        <FlatList
          data={arrayOfImages}
          renderItem={renderItem}
          keyExtractor={(item) => item.id}
          showsVerticalScrollIndicator={false}
        />
      </View>
    );
  };
};
```

The surface component called `Feed` should only concern itself with importing the correct children components and general styling. It looks like this:

```
// src/surfaces/Feed.js

export const Feed = () => {
  const headerHeight = useHeaderHeight();

  return (
    <SafeAreaView
        style={{ flex: 1, paddingTop: headerHeight + 20,
          paddingHorizontal: 20 }}
    >
      <View>
        <ListOfAvatars />
        <ListOfCards />
      </View>
    </SafeAreaView>
  );
};
```

And the **Feed** surface of our app should look like this:

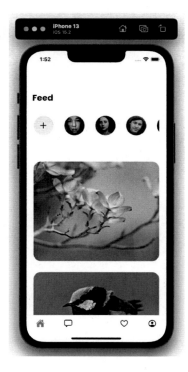

Figure 4.1 – An iPhone simulator screenshot of the Feed surface

You can leave your app as is, or you can copy some styling tweaks that I added in the GitHub repo. We're not focusing on styles in this book, so we're not going to go over them in detail; nonetheless, I encourage you to have a look around.

The **Feed** surface is looking quite similar to the design, so we can move forward to the **Conversations** surface.

Our **Conversations** surface needs to be wrapped in a new navigator because we want our users to be able to go into the conversation details. We'll add a new component called `<ConversationsNavigation>`, where we will create a Stack Navigator:

```
// src/surfaces/ConversationsNavigation.js

import React from "react";
import { Conversations } from "./Conversations";
```

```
import { Messages } from "./Messages";
import { createStackNavigator } from "@react-navigation/stack";

const Stack = createStackNavigator();

export const ConversationsNavigation = () => {
  return (
    <Stack.Navigator
      screenOptions={{
        //...
      }}
    >
        <Stack.Screen name='Conversations'
          component={Conversations} />
      <Stack.Screen
        name='Messages'
        component={Messages}
        options={({ route }) => ({
          title: route.params.name,
          //...
        })}
      />
    </Stack.Navigator>
  );
};
```

The most interesting option we're setting in this component is this one:

```
options={({ route }) => ({
        title: route.params.name,
        //...
```

This line of code tells **React Navigation** to use a route parameter as the header title for the `Messages` surface. If you test your app now, you will notice this is not happening yet. We also need to set this parameter at the time the user will choose to go to the `Messages` surface, which means we need to set it when `Conversation` is clicked. We will create the `Conversations` surface with an input box at the top, followed by a list of conversations in `FlatList`. Each item in the list will be wrapped in a `<Pressable>` component, which will look like this:

```
<Pressable onPress={() => navigation.navigate("Messages", {
  name: item.name })} >
```

When our users choose a conversation, this conversation will pass the assigned `name` parameter to the `Messages` surface, which in turn will display this name as the header. We can now add a list of dummy messages and conditional styling, which will style differently messages from the user and to the user. A useful thing to remember for message lists is to use the `inverted` prop on the `FlatList` component of messages. After all, we want the latest item to appear at the bottom of the list.

You may notice at this point that the `Conversations` surface and the `Messages` surface do not have the bottom tabs visible. The best way to achieve this functionality is to move our `<ConversationsNavigation>` out of the tab navigator and move it into the main stack navigator. The surfaces listed in the main stack will be displayed above the surfaces in the Tab Navigator, plus we will be able to use the pre-configured back button provided by the React Navigation library. Here's what the `App.js` root component should look like:

```
// src/App.js

export default function App() {
  //...
  return (
    <SafeAreaProvider>
      <NavigationContainer>
        <Stack.Navigator>
          {!userLoggedIn ? (
            <Stack.Screen name='Login' component={Login} />
          ) : (
            <>
              <Stack.Screen
                name='Home'
                component={Home}
                options={{ headerShown: false }}
              />
```

```
            <Stack.Screen
              name='ConversationsNav'
              component={ConversationsNavigation}
              options={{ headerShown: false }}
            />
          </>
        )}
      </Stack.Navigator>
    </NavigationContainer>
  </SafeAreaProvider>
);
}
```

In order to have a button for our **Conversations** surface displayed in the tabs, we will need to create an empty dummy surface and pass it into the Tab Navigator:

```
// src/surfaces/Home.js

<Tab.Screen name='Feed' component={Feed} />
    <Tab.Screen
      name='ConversationsMain'
        component={ConversationsBase} // just a dummy
          component which will never be called
      options={{
        tabBarIcon: ({ size }) => (
            <Ionicons name='chatbox-outline' color='#000000'
              size={size} />
        ),
      }}
      listeners={({ navigation }) => ({
        tabPress: (e) => {
          e.preventDefault();
          navigation.navigate("ConversationsNav");
        },
      })}
    />
    <Tab.Screen name='AddPost' component={AddPost} />
// …
```

We'll add a floating button at the bottom of the **Conversations** surface, and we're done!

I'm going over these code changes fairly quickly, because we don't want to spend too much time focusing on styling or React Navigation tips and tricks. We want to be up and running with an app that's close to something you may find in the real world, so we can start playing with state and data management. Feel free to go over all code changes in the GitHub repo, where you can also ask questions and raise issues.

We'll continue our progress by adding content to the **Favorites** surface. This will be a list of cards, like what can be found on the **Feed** surface. Next, we'll add components to the **Profile** surface. We will need an avatar, a name, some statistics, and two `FlatList` components that will display added images and favorited images.

We will finish up this surface by adding a custom component to the `Tab Navigator` for the central item, the black button for adding posts. We can add any custom component that we want as the tab bar icon:

```
// src/surfaces/Home.js
function Home() {
  return (
    <Tab.Navigator>
//…
    <Tab.Screen
        name='AddPost'
        component={AddPost}
        options={{
          tabBarIcon: ({ size }) => (
            <View
              style={{
                marginTop: -30,
              }}
            >
              <View
                style={{
                  position: "absolute",
                  backgroundColor: "#000000",
                  padding: 30,
                  bottom: -10,
                  left: -13,
                  borderRadius: 23,
```

```
                    transform: [{ rotate: "-45deg" }],
                    shadowColor: "#000000",
                    shadowOffset: { width: 0, height: 4 },
                    shadowOpacity: 0.2,
                    shadowRadius: 4,
                  }}
              />
                  <Ionicons name='add-circle-outline'
                  color='#ffffff' size={36} />
            </View>
          ),
        }}
      />
  //...
```

If you look closely, you will notice that the styling for this button is very similar to the floating button on the `Conversations` surface. In cases where we're repeating a lot of code, it's a good idea to abstract it into a separate file. This is called **Don't Repeat Yourself** (**DRY**) programming. We don't want to go too far, making abstractions for every little thing. There's another programming principle called **Write Everything Twice** (**WET**) programming, which advocates writing verbose code, especially when starting a new project. My personal preference is **Avoid Hasty Abstractions** (**AHA**) programming, proposed by *Kent C. Dodds*. This approach marries DRY and WET principles and encourages us programmers to find the best use cases for abstractions while not overusing them.

In this specific case, we are repeating styling. We can easily create a class called something like `floatingButton` and apply it to both of our components. We could also use the **Styled Components** library and create a `<FloatingButton>` styled component. There are more ways to achieve this goal of having reusable styles, but we are not going to dive into them. I'll do some cleanup in our components, and I'll meet you right back here in a few moments so that we can hook up some real data from our (almost) real API.

Pulling in data for the app

Welcome back! Did you take a moment to look at our app code? Did you clone the repo from the `chapter-3` branch, or did you create your own components following the broad strokes I described previously? Either way, I'm glad you're here! Let's fetch some data and use some state!

A quick reminder about the data we'll be using: I set up GitHub Pages in the /docs folder, which you can find here: https://github.com/PacktPublishing/Simplifying-State-Management-in-React-Native/tree/main/docs.

You can preview every JSON file right in the GitHub UI. You can also view the raw contents of any file by clicking the **Raw** button:

Figure 4.2 – GitHub UI with the Raw button circled in red

The text file visible after clicking this button is what you could see as an API response.

We'll start with fetching the list of users. This list contains user IDs and links to user avatars. Our API depends on us to manage the user avatars everywhere in the app and passes them in this one endpoint only.

So, let's check where we need the list of users. We need it on the **Feed** surface to display the list of avatars. We will also need it to display avatars on the cards on the **Feed** surface. We will also need the user data on the **Conversations** surface and the **Messaging** surface. At this point, it will be beneficial to find the common parent of those surfaces and call our API in the said parent. In our case, the parent is the root component declared in App.js.

The first thing we'll do is fetch our data in the parent:

```
// src/App.js

export default function App() {
  const [userLoggedIn, setIsUserLoggedIn] = useState(true);
  const [userList, setUserList] = useState(null);

//…

  async function fetchUserData(id) {
    const response = await fetch(requestBase + "/users.json");
    setUserList(await response.json());
```

```
}

useEffect(() => {
  fetchUserData();
}, []);

//...

if (!userList) {
  return <AppLoading />;
}
```

Once we have our data fetched and inside the `userList` object, we can pass it as a prop from the parent component to the children. According to the React Navigation docs, you can pass additional props through the render callback of the navigator. Here's what it would look like for the Home component:

```
<Stack.Screen name='Home' options={{ headerShown: false }}>
    {(props) => <Home {...props} userList={userList} />}
</Stack.Screen>
```

Once we have the `userList` prop in the Home surface, we should be done, yes? Unfortunately, no. The Home surface is a parent for the tab navigator, so we need to do the whole song and dance of adding the render callback for the Feed surface. Once we get to the Feed surface, we will need to pass the `userList` prop to the `ListOfAvatars` component… This is starting to be a bit much, don't you think? This is a taste of what would be called prop drilling in a bigger app. Passing an object through multiple surfaces and components is not only tedious but also error-prone. This sort of setup is brittle – it suffices that one component in the chain changes, and the whole app may become unusable. What can we do to avoid this? We can use **React Context**. This is also the strategy recommended by the maintainers of React Navigation.

> **What is context?**
> Context is used to pass data down the component tree without having to thread the props manually through every component.

The first step we need to take is to create our context with an initial value:

```
const UserListContext = React.createContext(null);
```

Then, we need to wrap the parent component in a Context Provider with an updated value:

```
// src/App.js
return (
    <SafeAreaProvider>
        <UserListContext.Provider value={{ userList: userList }}>
            <NavigationContainer theme={MyTheme}>
                <Stack.Navigator>
//…
```

The last piece of the context puzzle is how to use it, or "consume it." Once the context is provided to the parent, we can consume it in any one of its children through the `<Context.Consumer>` component. We will add this consumer to our list of avatars:

```
// src/components/ListOfAvatars.js

export const ListOfAvatars = () => {
  const renderItem = ({ item }) => {
   //…
  };
  return (
    <UserListContext.Consumer>
      {({ userList }) => (
          <View
          //…
          >
            <FlatList
              data={userList}
              renderItem={renderItem}
              keyExtractor={ (item) => item.id}
              horizontal
              //…
```

And there we go! We successfully fetched external data, fed it to our app, and passed the data around with the help of React Context. Using context offers a much better developer experience; however, it does come with its own set of issues. The biggest issue that you should always keep in mind when using context is that any change to the context will cause a re-render of the component where the `Provider` is placed, along with all the children of the said component. This means that if we were to have an API where the user can add or remove other users to their list, every time they would do this, the entire app would have to re-render. Sometimes, that's what we want; we want to have the avatar list and the list of images in Feed updated. We also want to update the Conversations surface in such a case. But what about the Profile and Add Post surfaces? We will not be answering those questions now, as we're working with an example app. However, every time you decide to use React's Context, you should ask yourself where to place the Provider and what will happen when the data of the context changes.

Let's continue fetching real data for other parts of our app. We'd like to display images on Feed. We'll start by fetching data in the ListOfCards component with a useEffect hook:

```js
// src/components/ListOfCards.js
import AppLoading from "expo-app-loading";
import { requestBase } from "../utils/constants";

export const ListOfCards = () => {
  const [cardList, setCardList] = useState(null);

  async function fetchCardData() {
    const response = await fetch(requestBase + "/home.json");
    setCardList(await response.json());
  }

  useEffect(() => {
    fetchCardData();
  }, []);

  if (!cardList) {
    return <AppLoading />;
  }
  return (
  //…
      <FlatList
        data={cardList.listOfitems}
        renderItem={renderItem}
        keyExtractor={ (item) => item.itemId}
```

Once our card items are fetched and passed on to the Card component, we can do something more with them – namely, we can check the author ID against the user list in our context and display the correct username and avatar thanks to this information.

We will add the same context consumer to the Card component as the one we added to ListOfAvatars, but that is not going to be enough in this case. Once we get the whole list, we also need to find the user whose ID matches the author ID of the card. We'll adjust the way we pass the context value, and we'll filter the userList array:

```
// src/components/Card.js
import { UserListContext } from "../context";

export const Card = ({ item }) => {
  return (
    <UserListContext.Consumer>
      {({ userList }) => {
        const currentUser = userList.filter(
          (user) => user.id === item.authorId
        );
        return (
          <View>
            <Image
            //…
```

We created a variable called currentUser, which is an array holding precisely one item – the user who posted the specific card. Unfortunately, this variable is accessible to the Card component only. If we wanted to use the same information, for example, on a modal that would open when we tap the image, we would have to either nest the modal component in the Card component or search for the current user again. You will see an example of this issue in our very own app in a few moments, when we'll be working with the Conversations surface.

On the other hand, we have composed another surface using the Card component – the Favorites surface. All we must do to have it working correctly is fetch the Favorites data. All the rest should fall into place.

If you encounter any problems with loading data from our example API hosted on GitHub pages, start by making sure the data is fetched. You can do so by using console.log in your code and looking in the terminal to see whether the object is fetched or not. Then, you need to check whether you have all the names and object keys spelled and nested correctly. If you get stuck at any point, remember that you can always go to the repo hosted on GitHub, clone it, and look around at any stage you would like.

Let's move on to the next component that needs to fetch data – Conversations. As I mentioned before, we will need to tweak and repeat some code we already wrote for the Card component used in the Feed and Favorites surfaces. In Conversations, we will also fetch the user list and search for the current user. Make sure to spell everything correctly. The sneaky API author named everything differently! Here's what my Conversations component looks like:

```
// src/components/ConversationItem.js
export const ConversationItem = ({ navigation, item }) => {
  return (
    <UserListContext.Consumer>
      {({ userList }) => {
        const currentUser = userList.filter((user) =>
          user.id === item.userId);
        return (
          <Pressable
          onPress={() =>
            navigation.navigate("Messages", {
              name: currentUser[0].name,
              avatar: currentUser[0].url,
            })
          }
          style={{
            height: 103,
        //...
```

Please pay attention to [0] after currentUser. We used a filter function on an array, and we have an array as a result. Omitting [0] means the app will not be displaying any data because it will see an array instead of an object.

We have our list of conversations; now's the time to fetch the specific conversation when one is tapped by the user. The action of redirecting to the messages screen happens in the <ConversationItem> component in FlatList on the Conversations surface. The Messages surface is a part of the same stack navigator as the Conversations, which means we could go two ways here:

1. Add context to the <ConversationsNavigation> component, set its value when a conversation is tapped, and consume it on the Messaging surface.

2. Pass the conversation ID as a route parameter, along with user data.

The second approach is very tempting because it's simple. We're just adding a piece of data that's already accessible to us, and we're passing it through the navigation to the correct place. There's nothing inherently wrong with this approach that I could criticize off the bat. It is foreseeable, however, that in a real-world app, you would end up writing very big or duplicated objects to be passed around in the `route` params. As per the React Navigation documentation, even though using route params is convenient, they should not be used as a replacement for a global app state. Manually passing data through route params can lead to bugs and an app showing outdated data. If you'd like a little bit of exercise, you could implement this solution in your own copy of the `FunBook` app right now.

When you're ready, come back here and I'll walk you through creating and consuming the new context for the conversations.

We'll start like before, by creating the context with its initial value:

```
export const ConversationContext = React.createContext(null);
```

I've decided to hold the functions to create context in a separate file, called `context.js` for simplicity's sake. Once the context is created, we need to wrap it around the correct component. In this case, we will need to add the Provider around the nested `Stack Navigator` of the `Conversations` surface. Let's add the following code to the `<ConversationsNavigation>` component:

```
// src/surfaces/ConversationsNavigation.js

import { ConversationContext } from "../context";

//…

export const ConversationsNavigation = () => {
  const [conversationId, setConversationId] = useState(null);
  return (
    <ConversationContext.Provider
      value={{
        conversationId: conversationId,
        setConversationId: setConversationId,
      }}
    >
      <Stack.Navigator
        screenOptions={{
          headerBackTitleVisible: false,
// …
```

You will notice we are passing both the value and the `setter` function to the context this time. This is because we will need to set the value of the context deeper in the tree, in the `<ConversationItem>` component. Not to worry though; passing functions through context is 100% a-okay!

What about multiple contexts, you may ask, when you notice that `<ConversationItem>` is already wrapped in `<UserListContext.Consumer>`? Again, this is totally fine. You can have just as many wrappers as you need and like! Here's what our component with two contexts will look like:

```js
// src/components/ConversationItem.js

export const ConversationItem = ({ navigation, item }) => {
  const onPressItem = (setConversationId, currentUser) => {
    setConversationId(item.id);

    navigation.navigate("Messages", {
      name: currentUser[0].name,
      avatar: currentUser[0].url,
    });
  };
  return (
    <ConversationContext.Consumer>
      {({ setConversationId }) => (
        <UserListContext.Consumer>
          {({ userList }) => {
            const currentUser = userList.filter(
              (user) => user.id === item.userId
            );
            return (
              <Pressable
                onPress={() => onPressItem(setConversationId,
                  currentUser)}
              //...
```

Now that we're setting the context, let's consume it in the `Messages` surface. We need to first get the conversation ID from the context and then fetch the correct JSON file for the given conversation. We'll add `<ConversationContext.Consumer>` as a wrapper on the `Messages` surface:

```js
// src/surfaces/Messages.js
```

```
export const Messages = ({ route }) => {
  const headerHeight = useHeaderHeight();

  return (
      <SafeAreaView style={{ flex: 1, paddingTop: headerHeight
        + 100 }}>
      <ConversationContext.Consumer>
        {(({ conversationId }) => (
```

Once we get the conversation ID, we'll use it in the `ListOfMessages` component to fetch the data pertinent to the given screen:

```
// src/components/ListOfMessages.js

import AppLoading from "expo-app-loading";
import { requestBase } from "../utils/constants";

export const ListOfMessages = ({ conversationId }) => {
  const [messages, setMessages] = useState(null);

  async function fetchMessages() {
    const response = await fetch(
      requestBase + "/messages/" + conversationId + ".json"
    );
    setMessages(await response.json());
  }

  useEffect(() => {
    fetchMessages();
  }, []);
  if (!messages) {
    return <AppLoading />;
  }

  const renderItem = ({ item }) => {
    //…
  };
```

```
return (
  //…
    <FlatList
      data={messages.messages}
      renderItem={renderItem}
      keyExtractor={(item) => item.id}
      showsVerticalScrollIndicator={false}
      inverted
    />
  </View>
  //…
```

And there we go! We've done some solid work here; it's time for a pat on the back. We have multiple components fetching data and passing it around when necessary. We've set up the Feed component, Favorites, Conversations, and Messaging. The last surface left is Profile. I will leave it to you, dear reader, to manage data on this surface. I trust that you have learned enough in this chapter to be able to do it on your own.

When you go to the book repo, you will find all work related to this chapter on a branch called chapter-3. You can browse through commits to see how the app development progressed, or you can simply check out the final state of the app. In the next chapter, we will see whether we can replace all our context, props, and filtering users with a more global solution called Redux. Onward and upward!

Summary

We have done a lot of great work in this chapter! There's a very specific sort of satisfaction when you see an app that looks nice and works smoothly, isn't there?

Here's where we are at after this chapter – we have an app that's styled according to design. This app pulls in external data from an API. I admit that our app is rather simple. There are many more functionalities that could be added to a social media clone app. And there's nothing stopping you from doing just that. You can play around and add and delete whatever you want. I will also add a few more functionalities, maybe a modal, or a functioning "like" button, and I'll see you in *Chapter 5*, where we'll start investigating our first state management solution – Redux.

Further reading

- `https://www.digitalocean.com/community/tutorials/what-is-dry-development`: DRY programming.

- `https://betterprogramming.pub/when-dry-doesnt-work-go-wet-6befda0444bf`: WET programming.

- `https://kentcdodds.com/blog/aha-programming`: AHA programming.

- `https://reactnavigation.org/docs/hello-react-navigation/#passing-additional-props`: Passing additional props in React Navigation.

- `https://reactjs.org/docs/context.html`: React Context.

- `https://reactnavigation.org/docs/params/#what-should-be-in-params`: React Navigation – what should be in params?

Part 3 – Exploring Various Libraries for State Management in React Native

In this part, we will start with Redux and its Toolkit; we will learn why they were created, how to configure them, and how to use them for managing liked images in the example app. Next, we will learn about MobX, what problems it wants to solve, and how to configure it and use it to manage liked images in the Funbook app. Then, we will learn about XState, what the mathematical bases for this library are, how to configure it, and how to visualize data thanks to its Visualizer. Finally, we will implement it for managing liked images in the Funbook app. Next comes Jotai; we will see why it was created and what problems it solves. Then, we will configure it for the Funbook app and use it to manage liked images. Finally, we will learn about React Query (or TanStack Query). We will learn why this library is even mentioned in a book about state management. Then, we will configure it and use it for fetching liked images in the Funbook app.

This part includes the following chapters:

- *Chapter 5, Implementing Redux in Our Funbook App*
- *Chapter 6, Using MobX as a State Manager in a React Native App*
- *Chapter 7, Untangling Complex Flows in React Native Apps with XState*
- *Chapter 8, Integrating Jotai in a React Native App*
- *Chapter 9, Using React Query for Server-Side - Driven State Management*

5

Implementing Redux in Our Funbook App

In the previous chapter, we got our hands "dirty" a little bit. I hope you liked building the Funbook app! We managed to build the frontend of a functioning app. Of course, the functionalities we created were limited. A real-world social media app would be much more robust, with many more components and user flows. However, bigger apps bring their own set of problems: handling large datasets, establishing style guides, managing analytics, and many other problems that we don't want to spend our time on. We are here to talk about different solutions for state management. In the interest of staying focused, I added a few functionalities to our app that were not described in detail in the previous chapter. I added a modal displaying an enlarged version of the images on the **Feed** surface, another modal displaying images added by the users listed at the top of the **Feed** surface and components and styles for the **Login** surface, and a functioning **Like** button in the modal with the images, connected to the **Profile** surface. You can find the full example app in the `example-app-full` folder on GitHub:

`https://github.com/PacktPublishing/Simplifying-State-Management-in-React-Native/tree/main/example-app-full`.

This app will be the base for all our state management experiments throughout this book. We will start our experiments by looking at the oldest state management library: **Redux**.

In this chapter, we will do the following:

- Go over a brief history of **Redux**
- Install and configure **Redux** in the Funbook app
- Add **Redux** functionalities to the app
- Learn about debugging **Redux**

By the end of this chapter, you should feel comfortable using **Redux**-specific jargon, such as reducer, actions, and store. You should also have a good understanding of what it takes to configure and use **Redux** in a real **React Native** app.

Technical requirements

In order to follow along with this chapter, you will need some knowledge of JavaScript and ReactJS. If you have followed the previous two chapters of this book, you should be able to go forward without any issues.

Feel free to use an IDE of your choice, as React Native does not need any specific functionality. Currently, the most popular IDEs for frontend developers are Microsoft's VSCode, Atom, Sublime Text, and WebStorm.

The code snippets provided in this chapter are here to illustrate what we should be doing with the code. They do not provide the whole picture. To code along easier, please open the GitHub repo in your IDE and look at the files in there. You can either start with the files in the folder named `example-app-full` or `chapter-5`. If you start with `example-app-full`, you will be responsible for implementing the solutions described in this chapter. If you choose to look at `chapter-5`, you will see the entire solution implemented by me.

If you get stuck or lost, you can check the code in the GitHub repo:

`https://github.com/PacktPublishing/Simplifying-State-Management-in-React-Native/tree/main/chapter-5`.

What is Redux? A brief history

We went over a brief history of **React** in *Chapter 1, What are React and React Native?*. If you skipped that chapter, or simply don't remember, don't worry. All you need to know is that **ReactJS** was published in 2013 and it opened doors to creating beautiful single-page applications. **ReactJS** was an exciting library to use! A lot of people jumped on the opportunity and started re-writing their websites. As time passed, many developers would discover that creating and maintaining large applications with **ReactJS** became tedious. Don't forget this was happening before the **ReactJS** team introduced hooks and context. Developers had to pass props from parents to nested children, going through multiple levels of irrelevant components. This is called **prop** drilling, as getting to the child component through many ancestors feels like drilling.

In 2015, something very interesting happened: *Dan Abramov* and *Andrew Clark* wrote and published a new open source library called Redux. ReactJS developers were mostly confused at first, given that **Redux** introduced new concepts to the **ReactJS** world. We could start thinking about global states that are accessible from anywhere in the app. In order to change a global state, we would need to use special functions called "actions" and also use something called "reducers"... This was a lot to take in! Regardless, this new library solved a very real problem, so the only thing to do was to buckle up, watch Dan Abramov's tutorials, and use this new and amazing tool!

Thanks to Dan Abramov's efforts to teach, explain, and popularize **Redux**, it became a staple of **ReactJS** development. As years passed, new concepts for managing global states were created, some similar and some very different from **Redux**. Compared to the newer solutions, **Redux** can feel clunky, as it has a large amount of boilerplate code. Even the library author expressed his doubts through Twitter:

Figure 5.1 – Dan Abramov's tweet saying he does not understand the Redux example code

Around 2016, the maintenance of **Redux** was passed to *Mark Erikson* and *Tim Dorr*. I had the chance to exchange a few messages with Mark Erikson. He explained to me that he's not getting paid for maintaining **Redux**; he does it in his spare time, even though it can be very time-consuming. He says himself that he became a **Redux** maintainer by accident, but after reading his excellent blog post on this topic, I would say he became a **Redux** maintainer because of the amazing amount of work he put into **Redux** documentation and the time he spent helping developers who use **Redux**. You can read the full story on his blog (link in the *Further reading* section). Mark added that he likes maintaining **Redux**. He butts heads with developers who are unhappy with the decisions he's making sometimes, but he also receives support from fellow OSS maintainers, as well as conference invites. I asked Mark what he thinks about **Redux**'s place in the current state management libraries landscape. He pointed out there are many resources (NPM statistics, GitHub statistics, etc.) proving that **Redux** is still by far the most widely used state management library with **React** apps. However, as Mark said, **Redux** was heavily over-used from 2016 to 2017. During that time, a lot of developers raised legitimate complaints about the size of **Redux**'s boilerplate. This situation led in turn to a backlash on Twitter, where a lot of people made claims that "**Redux** is dead" because one tool or another "killed it."

"**RTK** and **React-Redux** hooks changed that narrative. If you look at discussions on Reddit and Twitter today, you do see a good number of folks saying how much they love RTK and recommending it," Mark said.

Redux is currently a mature and trusted solution for managing global states in **React** and **React Native** apps. We've looked briefly at its history in this section. It is obvious that it has its shortcomings. To quote Mark Erikson, "This is a useful tool, not meant for every situation, but a very valid choice." It has its fans and haters, but it's worth knowing about – and that's why we're here! Let's go!

Installing and configuring Redux

As with any library that we would like to add to our project, we will start by reading the documentation. The **Redux** documentation has evolved a lot over the years. In 2022, the recommended install includes **Redux Toolkit**.

Redux Toolkit is the recommended official approach to using **Redux**. It contains commonly used packages and dependencies for building **Redux** apps. This toolkit also simplifies a lot of tasks necessary for using **Redux**, such as creating the store or reducers. Any user is free to install and use core **Redux**, but we will use the recommended approach and use **Redux Toolkit**.

> **Why not just Redux?**
>
> The Redux library has evolved a lot since its conception in 2015. Its ecosystem has also grown a lot. The recommended Redux Toolkit is the most practical addition to Redux apps written in 2022, although it is not a necessity.

Let's start by going into the files for the full app, which is placed in the `example-app-full` folder. Feel free to work directly on those files on your computer. You can also fork the repository or copy the files from this folder. These files include everything you need to run a complete app. If you prefer to follow along with the working code, you should look in the `chapter-5` folder. That is where all completed work for this chapter is placed.

Let's get started. Follow these steps:

1. Once you are inside the `app` folder, run the following command:

    ```
    npm install @reduxjs/toolkit
    ```

    We will go ahead and install the complementary packages recommended in the Redux documentation.

2. Let's run the following commands:

    ```
    npm install react-redux
    npm install --save-dev @redux-devtools/core
    ```

    Now that the dependencies are installed, we can take a minute to talk about **Redux** core concepts.

The main concept, and the absolute most important one, is that with **Redux**, we consider the state a plain object. The **Redux** documentation uses a to-do app as an example, but we can go ahead and use our Funbook app.

If we were to represent the state of the logged-in user of the Funbook app with a single object, it may look something like this:

```
{
    userLoggedIn: true,
    userData: {
        id: 3,
        name: "John Doe",
        email: "john@doe.com",
        image: "imageURL",
        addedImages: [...],
        likedImages: [...],
        numberOfPosts: 35,
        numberOfFollowers: 1552,
        numberOfFollows: 128,
        idsOfFollowedUsers: [...],
        idsOfConversations: [...]
    },
}
```

In this example, we are trying to figure out holistically what user data will be necessary for the entire app. This is what is considered the GLOBAL state. We are not going surface to surface; we want to know all the data relevant to the user. Therefore, in the `userData` object here, you will find data such as the username and email, which will be used on the **Profile** surface, an array of IDs of followed users, which we can use on the **Feed** surface for the list of avatars, and the array of IDs of conversations necessary for the **Conversations** surface.

Of course, not all our app data is directly dependent on the logged-in user. Let's try and imagine the shape of the part of our global state for the modals present on the `Feed` surface. Here's what the state of the modal opened on an image click may look like:

```
{
    imageModalOpen: true,
    imageId: 3,
    authorId: 3,
    imageUrl: "imageUrl",
    numberOfLikes: 28,
    numberOfConversations: 12,
    numberOfFollows: 128
}
```

Going around the app, we may want to consider the shape of the slice of a global state related to the **Conversations** surface. In my opinion, the data shape we fetch from the fake API set up on GitHub Pages fits very well with the shape of the global state:

```
[
  {
    "id": 1,
    "userId": 2,
    "text": "Hey, how's it going?"
  },
  {
    "id": 2,
    "userId": 4,
    "text": "Yo, are you going to the wedding?"
  },
  //...
```

Having the global state be the same shape as the API response is generally welcome. In these cases, you, as the frontend developer, will not have to reshape the data or remember what keys are used where and why. In a perfect world, the API responses would always fit the shape of the data necessary to be shown on the UI. However, in the real world, that may mean that the frontend would be unnecessarily fetching data that can be shared between surfaces, or fetching unnecessarily big datasets or images.

I feel we are getting the hang of this whole idea of a global state, right? Feel free to try and figure out on your own what other slices of the global state our app may need. Maybe you can sketch out the shape of the global state necessary for the modal displayed when an avatar is pressed – or maybe what exactly is needed for the `Favorited` images surface, and the same data on the `Profile` surface. Come back here when you feel ready to move on to the second **Redux** concept: dispatching actions.

Oh hi! You're back! Great! Let's talk more about **Redux** then!

Dispatching actions

Let's say we've set up the global state – we replaced a lot of unnecessary props and we're happy – but what if we want to change something? What if the user likes an image? What if the user adds a new image or follows another user? We need to tell our state that something has changed. This is when we will dispatch actions. An action is a plain JavaScript object that describes what is happening. We could dispatch an action that looks like this:

```
{ type: 'LIKE_IMAGE', payload: { Object with data about the
liked image } }
```

What now? Has the global state changed magically? Unfortunately, no. We still need to tell **Redux** to change the state based on this action. The missing piece of this puzzle that ties the actions to the state is called a reducer. Reducer functions are plain **JavaScript** functions that take in the old state and the action and return the new state of the app. Here's what a very simple reducer for liked images may look like:

```
function likedImages(state =[], action) {
  if (action.type === 'LIKE_IMAGE') {
    let newLikedImages = state;
    newLikedImages.push(action.payload);
    return newLikedImages
  } else {
    return state
  }
}
```

We are taking in the old state – in this case, the array of liked images. We are then adding the new item and returning the new state. We also get some very elegant error handling in the `else` block, where if there are any problems, the app will return to the old state.

I have described three concepts in this section:

1. **The store** – the single source of truth for the global state
2. **Reducers** – functions that take in the old state and the action, do what you need them to do, and return the new state
3. **Actions** – plain JavaScript objects containing information for the store

These are basically all you need to know to start using **Redux** effectively. If you would like to read more about the concepts and the history of this great library, check out the *Further reading* section where you'll find links to the **Redux** documentation. Now that we know the basics, we are ready to apply this fresh knowledge to a real app.

Adding Redux functionalities to the app

We have installed the **Redux Toolkit** with our friendly package manager in the previous section, but we haven't made any real changes in our app yet. We have, however, thought about the data flows in our app in the previous chapters. The work that we need to do now is going to be very similar. We will start by designing the state structure and actions. When we have both of those, we will add reducers to tie everything together.

There's a lot of work ahead of us, so let's try to break it down into smaller chunks. We will start by looking at the user state and how we could manage a user's logged-in and logged-out state with a global state in **Redux**. We will then do that same walkthrough for liked images in our app. When we have successfully set up those two pieces of the global state, we will look at how we can combine them and use them in our app. We will then create some actions to handle events in the app. Once we have the state and the actions, we'll take a brief look at how data can be fetched in an app with **Redux**. Finally, we will be ready to get rid of the **React** context we used before for managing the state of our app.

User login state walkthrough

Let's start with the user state. We will create a new file called `store.js` where we will store our initial state slices. We will add this **JavaScript** object to that file:

```
export const user = {
  userLoggedIn: false,
  userData: null,
};
```

When the app is first loaded, we will assume the user is not logged in and there is no user data.

Now, we need to think of an action that will be dispatched when the user is logging in. It should look like this:

```
{type: 'LOGIN', payload: userData}
```

The last part is the reducer. Let's create a new folder for our reducers, called… well, `reducers`. Inside this folder, we will create our reducer file, which should look like this:

```
// reducers/user.js
import { user } from "../store";

export const login = (state=user, action) => {
  if (action.type === 'LOGIN') {
    return {
        ...state,
        user: {
          userLoggedIn: true,
          user: action.payload,
        },
    }
  } else {
```

```
    return state
  }
}
```

We are importing our user object as the initial state and then we're adding a switch that will listen to specific actions. Let's listen to the `'LOGIN'` action.

But wait – what if our user would like to sign out? We need another action specifically for this:

```
{ type: 'LOGOUT' }
```

I didn't add any action payload in this case, because we will not be passing any actual data. We only want to wipe the data and we will do that in the reducer. We could add another 'if' statement to the reducer, but big `if-else` statements become difficult to read and reason about. In the case of reducers, it's a good idea to use the `switch` statement, since we're effectively switching between different states of the app. Here's what our reducer will look like:

```
export const login = (state=user, action) => {
  switch (action.type) {
    case "LOGIN": {
      return {
        ...state,
        user: {
          userLoggedIn: true,
          user: action.payload,
        },
      };
    }
    case "LOGOUT": {
      return {
        ...state,
        user: {
          userLoggedIn: false,
          user: null,
        },
      };
    }
    default:
```

```
        return state;
    }
}
```

OK – now when a user logs in, we will set the global state of the app to reflect that, right? Almost! We still need to find the right place in our code where we will dispatch this action, and that place is the login button on the **Login** surface – but our **Login** surface is shown based on the local state of the main component! That means there's still a little bit more work that we need to do before we will see the magic of Redux. Don't worry though, it will be worth it!

Important information

If you do have any doubts about all this extra work we seem to be doing, I invite you, my dear reader, to read the **React Navigation** documentation on authentication flows: `https://reactnavigation.org/docs/auth-flow/`. In this documentation, you will find that you should not manually navigate when conditionally rendering screens. You would also need to set up the context and preferably use the `useReducer` hook from **ReactJS**. If `useReducer` sounds familiar at this point, that is because it's a **ReactJS** hook with identical functionality to the **Redux** reducers. I hope by now you are starting to feel convinced that using a state management library such as **Redux** is a great solution for React Native apps.

You may wonder why we used a spread operator with the state and then changed the value of `userLoggedIn`. Theoretically, it would be easier to just change the value in the state, no? Not in **Redux**. **Redux** is very adamant about the reducers NOT being able to modify the current state. Reducers can only copy the state and make changes to the copied values. This is important so that our code is predictable. If many reducers changed the same slice of state, who's to say what would be the result?

Immutability

This is a very fancy word, isn't it? It means that something is not capable of change, or that it should not be changed. In the case of JavaScript apps, immutable data management can increase performance and make programming and debugging easier. Redux reducers take in the old state and the action and return a new state object; they should never apply changes to the "old" state object.

If you are curious about the key concepts of **Redux**, I invite you again to the *Further reading* section, where you will find a link to a free course on `Egghead.io`, created by the author of **Redux**, *Dan Abramov*.

Using Redux for liked images

Our global state is rather poor so far. Keeping the user data in the global state is great but we can surely do more with this great tool. How about liking posts? The reducer for liking posts will look like this:

```
export const likedImages = (state = [], action) => {
  if (action.type === "LIKE_IMAGE") {
    let newLikedImages = state;
    newLikedImages.push(action.payload);
    return newLikedImages;
  } else {
    return state;
  }
};
```

And what if the user decided to unlike a post? Let's add an action and a reducer for this scenario:

```
{ type: 'UNLIKE_IMAGE', payload: { Object with data about the
unliked image } }
```

Now, let's adjust our reducer. Since we have multiple actions in a single reducer, we will use a `switch` statement again:

```
// ./reducers/likedImages.js
export const likedImagesReducer = (state = [], action) => {
  switch (action.type) {
    case "LIKE_IMAGE": {
      const newLikedImage = action.payload;
      return [...state, newLikedImage];
    }
    case "UNLIKE_IMAGE": {
      const stateWithoutLikedImage = state.filter(
        (item) => item !== action.payload
      );
      return stateWithoutLikedImage;
    }
    default: {
      throw new Error(`Unhandled action type: ${action.type}`);
```

```
      }
    }
};
```

Combining various pieces of global state

We have two reducers, each one meant to manage two different actions. What we need to do now is create a store that will represent the global state of the Funbook app and pass actions into reducers. We could use the `createStore` function from core **Redux**, but that would require adding more boilerplate files and functions, and it is not the recommended approach for modern **Redux**. The recommended approach is using **Redux Toolkit**, which we will do right now. **Redux Toolkit** offers a special `configureStore` function, which will do a lot of heavy lifting for us. All we need to do is add this function:

```
// ./store.js
import { configureStore } from "@reduxjs/toolkit";

import usersReducer from "./reducers/users";
import likedImagesReducer from "./reducers/likedImages";

export const store = configureStore({
  reducer: {
    user: usersReducer,
    likedImages: likedImagesReducer,
  },
});
```

The `configureStore` function combined our two reducers for us, creating a root reducer required by **Redux**. This single root reducer is required to achieve a single source of truth in the app. This function also adds some useful middleware functionalities, which will check for common mistakes and expose our code for easier debugging.

We created the global state, and we configured it with the reducers thanks to **Redux Toolkit**. Now, we need to tell our Funbook app to use this state. In order to do so, we will use a `<Provider>` component wrapper provided (no pun intended) by the **Redux** library. If you paid attention while we were setting up the app without any exterior libraries, you will have noticed that the **React** context also uses `<Provider>` components. The naming convention is not an accident. Both `<Provider>` components serve the same purpose and **React** context uses a lot of the same high-level logic as **Redux**.

Let's import the necessary elements into our main app file, `App.js`:

```
import { store } from "./store";
import { Provider } from "react-redux";
```

And let's wrap our app in the Redux `<Provider>`:

```
export default function App() {
//...
  return (
    <SafeAreaProvider>
      <Provider store={store}>
//...
```

This looks familiar, doesn't it? **Redux**'s `<Provider>` shares a lot of similarities with **React's** context. I cannot give you any links to official blog posts from the Meta team where React maintainers officially explain this. I can, however, give you my personal opinion that the React team saw the solution that **Redux** was bringing to large **React** apps and thought that some of its principles were worth importing into the **React** repository itself. There are other state management solutions out there, obviously. If there weren't, I wouldn't be able to write this book! Regardless, **Redux** holds a special place in the React ecosystem.

After this short break, we will dive back into our code! We have our store and `Provider` set up. We also have two reducers ready: for user data and liked images data. Let's start with replacing the liked images. We'll go into the `surfaces` folder, where we will find the Favorited surface. This, in turn, will lead us to the component named `ListOfFavorites`, which displays data from the Favorited context.

We will remove this context and use **Redux** data. We will start by importing a `useSelector` hook from Redux, and then we will fetch the actual data from **Redux** using this hook:

```
// src/components/ListOfFavorites
import { useSelector } from "react-redux";

export const ListOfFavorites = ({ navigation }) => {
    const { likedImages } = useSelector((state) =>
      state.likedImages);
//...
```

Do you have our app running on your phone or in the simulator? I hope you do because then you will notice something just went very wrong!

Figure 5.2 – iPhone simulator screenshot with a Redux error

Unhandled action type…? I think I've seen this somewhere… Oh yes! That's the default in our `switch` statement in the `likedImages` reducer! This is not really the default that we want, so let's go ahead and change it so that it returns the initial state by default:

```
//reducers/likedImages.js
export const likedImagesReducer = (state = [], action) => {
  switch (action.type) {
  //…
```

```
    default: {
      return state;
    }
  }
};
```

The app loads correctly – we're back in business! We are passing the initial state as the default value to the `likedImages` reducer, which means we are passing an empty array – but we want to fetch image data. We did this before in the Context Providers using `fetch`. `FavoritedContextProvided` used React's `useReducer` hook along with an `init_likes` action dispatched when the images were fetched successfully. When it comes to **Redux**, we do not add functions inside `Provider`. We will create a fetching function inside an action, and then we will dispatch that action when the Favorited surface is rendered. This is a simplistic solution for a simple app. If you are working on a bigger app, you would probably need to concern yourself with caching, avoiding duplicate requests or a cache lifetime. In that case, you should look into a tool provided by Redux Toolkit, called RTK Query, which simplifies data fetching and caching in Redux apps.

> **A full toolbelt**
>
> It may start to feel overwhelming learning about so many tools at once. We started with Redux, continued with Redux Toolkit, and now we're adding RTK Query. Don't worry too much at this point about libraries and tool names. We're here to learn how to effectively write an app with a state managed by Redux, and we're following the documentation and best practices to do so. Once you're familiar with the suggested solution, feel free to look around the Redux ecosystem and find the approach that you like the most. There are no wrong answers when it comes to what you like and don't like!

Taking advantage of Redux Toolkit for creating actions

Our reducer is very limited so far. We can't use it directly to fetch data, because as the rules of reducers state, reducers cannot be used to do any asynchronous logic. If we were writing our app sometime around 2018 or 2019, we would probably create a separate `actions` file, manually configure **Redux** middleware functions to manage asynchronous API calls, and finally proceed to write the fetching actions. Luckily, in 2022, we can take advantage of Redux Toolkit, which comes bundled with all the necessary helper functions and a utility called `createSlice`. A "slice" in **Redux** lingo is a collection of reducers and actions for a single feature in your app. Let's convert our `likedImages` reducer into a **Redux** Toolkit slice:

```
//reducers/likedImages.js
import { createSlice } from "@reduxjs/toolkit";
```

```
export const likedImagesSlice = createSlice({
  name: "likedImages",
  initialState: [],
  reducers: {
    likeImage: (state) => {
      const newLikedImage = action.payload;
      return [...state, newLikedImage];
    },
    unLikeImage: (state, action) => {
      const stateWithoutLikedImage = state.filter(
        (item) => item !== action.payload
      );
      return stateWithoutLikedImage;
    },
  },
});

export const { init, likeImage, unLikeImage } =
likedImagesSlice.actions;

export default likedImagesSlice.reducer;
```

Fetching data

Since **Redux** was conceived as a state management tool, it did not come ready to manage fetching data out of the box – but, again, we are using **Redux Toolkit**, which is bundled with the necessary middleware that will let our Redux store digest fetched data. We will use the `createAsyncThunk` function from **Redux Toolkit**.

> **What's a thunk?**
> A thunk is a special sort of function that's returned by another function. This name is not related to **Redux** itself.

Here's what our fetching thunk will look like:

```
import { createAsyncThunk } from "@reduxjs/toolkit";
import { requestBase } from "./src/utils/constants";
```

```
export const fetchLikedImages = createAsyncThunk(
  "likedImages/initLikedImages",
  async () => {
    const response = await fetch(requestBase + "/john_doe/
      likedImages.json");
    return await response.json();
  }
);
```

Now, we need to tell our **Redux** slice about this function. We will use the extraReducers function provided by **Redux Toolkit** to keep our reducer clean and readable:

```
// reducers/likedImages.js
import { createSlice } from "@reduxjs/toolkit";
import { fetchLikedImages } from "../asyncFetches";

export const likedImagesSlice = createSlice({
  name: "likedImages",
  initialState: {
    likedImages: [],
    loading: true,
  },
  reducers: {
   //…
  },
  extraReducers: (builder) => {
    builder.addCase(fetchLikedImages.pending, (state) => {
      state.loading = true;
    });
      builder.addCase(fetchLikedImages.fulfilled,
        (state, action) => {
      state.likedImages = action.payload;
      state.loading = false;
    });
      builder.addCase(fetchLikedImages.rejected, (state) => {
      state.loading = false;
```

```
      });
    },
});
```

Now that we have a pretty elegant way to manage fetching, including a pending state and rejected state, let's actually fetch our data. We should not fetch it in the `ListOfFavorited` component, because we need to have the image data available as soon as the entire app is rendered. We should fetch the images in the parent component, `Home`:

```
//src/surfaces/Home
import { fetchLikedImages } from "../../asyncFetches";
import { useDispatch, useEffect } from "react-redux";
// ...
export const Home = () => {
  const dispatch = useDispatch();

  useEffect(() => {
    dispatch(fetchLikedImages());
  }, []);
```

This way, the liked images data will be fetched when the app is rendered and the user is on the **Feed** screen. Once the image data is fetched, we can read it from our global state in the `ListOfFavorites` component:

```
//src/components/ListOfFavorites
import { useSelector, useDispatch } from "react-redux";

export const ListOfFavorites = ({ navigation }) => {
    const { likedImages } = useSelector((state) =>
      state.likedImages);
  const dispatch = useDispatch();
  const [imageList, setImageList] = useState([]);

useEffect(() => {
    const reversedImages = [...likedImages].reverse();
    setImageList(reversedImages);
  }, [likedImages]);

 if (!imageList) {
    return <AppLoading />;
```

```
    }


//…
      <FlatList
        data={imageList}
        renderItem={renderItem}
        keyExtractor={(item) => item.itemId}
        //…
```

You may have noticed how the fetched data is passed to the state hook:

```
const reversedImages = [...likedImages].reverse();
```

We are using the ES6 spread operator in order to apply the `reverse()` function to a copy of the `likedImages` array. This is because the `likedImages` array is read-only and we cannot operate directly on it.

Replacing the context

Take a moment to look at what you have accomplished. You effectively replaced the Favorited context with Redux! The last thing we need to do is to replace the actions when an image is liked or not and then we'll be ready to do some cleanup!

Let's go into the `ImageDetailsModal` surface and replace context-related code with Redux code:

```
//src/surfaces/ImageDetailsModal
import { likeImage, unLikeImage } from "../../reducers/
  likedImages";
import { useDispatch, useSelector } from "react-redux";

export const ImageDetailsModal = ({ navigation, route }) => {
    const { likedImages } = useSelector((state) =>
      state.likedImages);
    const [isCurrentImageLiked, setIsCurrentImageLiked] =
useState(false);
    const dispatch = useDispatch();

    useEffect(() => {
      const checkIfLiked =
```

```
        likedImages?.filter(
            (favoritedImg) => favoritedImg.itemId ===
                route.params.imageItem.itemId
        ).length > 0;
    setIsCurrentImageLiked(checkIfLiked);
}, [likedImages]);
```

The last thing we need to change is the function called when the **Like** button is clicked on:

```
<Pressable
        onPress={() => {
          if (isCurrentImageLiked) {
            dispatch(unLikeImage(route.params.imageItem));
          } else {
            dispatch(likeImage(route.params.imageItem));
          }
        }}
      >
```

And we're done with applying **Redux** to the liked images! We can remove the `Favorited` context **Provider**.

Our app consists of functional components only, so we can use **Redux** hooks. If we had class components, we would have to wrap them with special functions called `mapStateToProps` and `mapDispatchToProps`. Modern **React** apps can be built without class components though – as you can see in the Funbook app.

In this section, you learned how to create a Redux store for the user state and liked images. We added reducers for both pieces of the store, as well as actions. We took advantage of a few utilities provided by Redux Toolkit to make our lives easier. We pulled it all together and were finally able to remove a little bit of React's context. Replacing all other pieces of context with **Redux** is a very good exercise to get the hang of this state management library. If you prefer to just take a look at what it would look like, check out the book repo and the folder: `https://github.com/PacktPublishing/Simplifying-State-Management-in-React-Native/tree/main/chapter-5-complete`.

We will now take a look at handling problems and debugging issues that may arise while using Redux.

Debugging

Our Funbook app is quite simple so far. However, when working with bigger apps you will notice that the state becomes more and more complicated with every added feature. Sometimes, features have overlapping states or complex actions, responsible for many things happening across the app. In order to hunt down bugs related to complex state changes, we can use a dedicated debugger. Configuring developer tools in a bare **Redux** app takes a couple of steps, but we're using **Redux Toolkit**! And it comes to the rescue yet again. **Redux Toolkit** is preconfigured to work with the **Redux** DevTools extension, which runs in the browser. Since we are working on a React Native app, we will need to use another tool, called **React Native** Debugger. Mac users can install it using the Homebrew tool:

```
brew install react-native-debugger
```

If you're not using a Mac computer, you will find a prebuilt binary of this app on their installation instructions page: https://github.com/jhen0409/react-native-debugger.

Once the remote Debugger is installed, you can run it by typing the following command into your Terminal:

```
open "rndebugger://set-debugger-loc?host=localhost&port=8081"
```

Since we are using **Expo**, there are a few changes we need to make to actually be able to debug our app. So far, the **React Native** Debugger tool with the default config has not found our app:

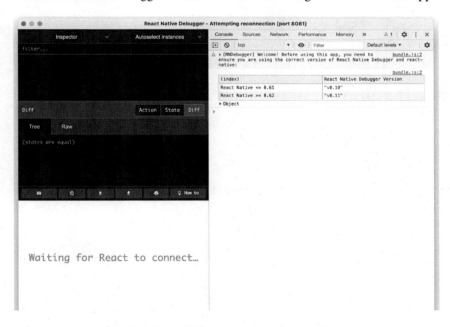

Figure 5.3 – React Native Debugger after installation

We need to tell **React Native** Debugger to look for the right port, which, in the case of **Expo**-managed apps, is `19000`. You will probably need to stop the debugger and the app, then run the following command to open React Native Debugger on the right port:

```
open "rndebugger://set-debugger-loc?host=localhost&port=19000"
```

Finally, restart the app by stopping the server in the Terminal and rerunning it as follows:

```
expo start
```

React Native Debugger is a very useful tool, not only for debugging Redux but also for inspecting all sorts of bugs in **React Native** apps.

In this section, we went over installing and using the **React Native** Debugger tool. I encourage you to look around this very useful tool, inspect the app, and maybe add some bad code to see what an error in this tool may look like.

Summary

We've come a long way on our journey through the state management ecosystem. In this chapter, we talked about what is considered the most common solution for state management in **React** apps – **Redux**. This library has gone through many changes itself. Using it in 2022 is quite different from how it was in 2016 thanks to **Redux Toolkit, which** we learned about. We talked about the **Redux** store, reducers, and actions. We've also implemented Redux for liked images in our Funbook app. We're now ready to compare this library to its descendant: **MobX**. In the next chapter, we will start by taking a brief look at the history and the high-level ideas behind **MobX**. We will then take `example-app-full` as our starting point and try to replace the `LikedImages` context as we did with **Redux**.

Further reading

- `https://redux.js.org/introduction/why-rtk-is-redux-today` – Why use Redux Toolkit?

- `https://redux.js.org/introduction/core-concepts` – Redux core concepts.

- `https://blog.isquaredsoftware.com/2016/09/how-i-got-here-my-journey-into-the-world-of-redux-and-open-source/` – Mark Erikson's blog on how he became a Redux maintainer.

- `https://blog.isquaredsoftware.com/2018/03/redux-not-dead-yet/` – Redux is not dead.

- `https://egghead.io/courses/fundamentals-of-redux-course-from-dan-abramov-bd5cc867` – Egghead tutorial by Dan Abramov.

- `https://stackoverflow.com/a/34582848/8798164` – Stack Overflow answer about state mutations.

- `https://redux.js.org/tutorials/essentials/part-2-app-structure#rules-of-reducers` – Rules of Reducers.

- `https://daveceddia.com/what-is-a-thunk/` – what is a thunk?

6

Using MobX as a State Manager in a React Native App

In the previous chapter, we had a chance to try the most popular state management solution in the **React** ecosystem – **Redux**. We looked in detail at replacing the `FavoritedImages` context with **Redux**. You can go back at any time to check what exactly was changed in the code in the GitHub repo's folder for *Chapter 5*: `https://github.com/PacktPublishing/Simplifying-State-Management-in-React-Native/tree/main/chapter-5`.

If you're curious to see the entire app fully migrated to Redux, please go to another folder: `https://github.com/PacktPublishing/Simplifying-State-Management-in-React-Native/tree/main/chapter-5-complete`.

We've had a steep hill to climb so far. We talked about **ReactJS**, **React Native**, and managing state without additional libraries, and finally, we looked at **Redux**. I can assure you, my dear reader, that if you were able to internalize the first five chapters of this book, the rest will be a breeze! All we will do now is the same exercise: replacing **ReactJS** context for `FavoritedImages` with a state management library. In this chapter, we will talk about **MobX**. We will start by taking a brief look at the history of MobX and learning about the concepts of MobX at a high level. After that, we will move on to configuring MobX in the Funbook app. Once we have the library set up in our project, we will move on to re-writing the `FavoritedImages` context with a MobX state, models, and actions.

Here's what this chapter will include:

- Going over **MobX** concepts
- Configuring **MobX** in the Funbook app
- Using **MobX** for `FavoritedImages`

By the end of this chapter, you should feel comfortable using **MobX**. Not only will you know what **MobX** models, snapshots, and stores are but you will also know whether you prefer them over **Redux**! And that's what this book is really about: getting to know different solutions so you can pick whichever you prefer for your future projects.

Technical requirements

In order to follow along with this chapter, you will need some knowledge of **JavaScript** and **ReactJS**. If you have followed at least *Chapters 1* to *4* of this book, you should be able to go forward without any issues.

Feel free to use an IDE of your choice, as React Native does not need any specific functionality. Currently, the most popular IDEs for frontend developers are Microsoft's VSCode, Atom, Sublime Text, and WebStorm.

The code snippets provided in this chapter are there to illustrate what we should be doing with the code. They do not provide the whole picture. To code along easier, please open the GitHub repo in your IDE and look at the files in there. You can either start with the file in the folder named `example-app-full` or `chapter-6`. If you start with `example-app-full`, you will be responsible for implementing the solutions described in this chapter. If you choose to look at `chapter-6`, you will see the entire solution implemented by me.

If you get stuck or lost, you can check the code in the GitHub repo: `https://github.com/PacktPublishing/Simplifying-State-Management-in-React-Native/tree/main/chapter-6`.

Going over MobX concepts

As you may have noticed, my dear reader, I like to start every big section with a little bit of history about the piece of software that we are going to examine. It so happens that MobX has a very calm presence in the React community. There isn't really any drama surrounding its conception or development. It was announced in 2015 as a solution on the blog of the company Mendix, where the creator of MobX, *Michel Weststrate*, used to work. The blog post details the reasons for creating this library, namely the fact that a pure ReactJS app in 2015 was not very good at managing complex states. Since then, MobX has been developed as an OSS library on GitHub. In 2016, it was joined by **MobX-State-Tree** (**MST**), a state container system for MobX. MST is to MobX what Redux Toolkit is to Redux. It's an additional tool made for a better **developer experience** (**DX**), but it's not required. I personally like to make my life easier, so in this book, we will use MST.

I exchanged a few messages with *Jamon Holmgren*, who is the CTO of Infinite Red, one of the most renowned software houses specializing in React Native, and the maintainer of **MST**. He said he found out about **MobX** around 5 years ago when his teammates were looking for alternatives to Redux. After doing a trial project, they really liked it and they've been using it ever since. It's even integrated into

Ignite, the **React Native** boilerplate by Infinite Red. Jamon says that "**MST's** main advantage is that you get the central store feel of Redux without having to touch four or five different files for every change. You also get granular re-renders without having to write a single selector and a very natural JavaScript-y feel. Developers at Infinite Red used MST on apps with hundreds of screens and millions of daily active users with little issue, so it's a proven state management system that works really well with React and React Native." In cases where developers have to work with less structured data, over which they need more control, **MobX** could be the better solution over **MST**.

"**MobX** still brings the observability (granular, targeted re-renders) and natural updates that MST has, but is much lighter weight," Jamon added.

MobX was created around 7 years ago, but it has stayed relevant over the years. Jamon says he would like to improve the **TypeScript** (**TS**) types of the library, but overall, he thinks the library is holding up very well thanks to its author's, Michel Westrate's, excellent engineering.

MobX is currently one of the most popular state management libraries for **React** apps. The documentation states that it's one of the most popular **Redux** alternatives. If you read the docs closely enough, you may find a few places where the authors allude to **MobX** being better than **Redux**. When I asked Jamon about this rivalry, he said, "It's always fun to have other great communities to banter with. The reality is that the **MobX** community respects the **Redux** community a ton. Their community pushes ours to be better and improve. They make different trade-off decisions and one or the other might not be your particular style, so it's great to have options."

The **MobX** maintainers have, of course, the full right to think the solution they are working on is better. Now, let's see what you think, my dear reader!

As far as **MobX** concepts and high-level ideas are concerned, there is one very important sentence underlined in the documentation:

> *Anything that can be derived from the application state, should be. Automatically.*

> *- The MobX Motto*

This is a new concept! Anything that can be derived, should be derived automatically. Have we derived anything from our app state automatically before? Not really. At first, we created `useState` and `useEffect` hooks, coupled with **React** context. We had to manually update all the necessary pieces of the state whenever the user interacted with our app. In Redux, we wrote out actions and they passed the information on state updates to the reducers. We may say the state update happened automatically; we didn't have to perform any additional tasks after passing the actions. We did, however, create the action and call it manually. We also know that **Redux** does not promote deriving values from the application state specifically. The **Redux** documentation concentrates more on immutability, the state being the single source of truth, and using plain functions.

The **MobX** documentation states that this library is based on transparent functional programming – a concept further explained in the book *MobX Quick Start Guide*, published by **Packt Publishing**. The philosophy of **MobX** is to be the following:

1. **Straightforward** – write minimalistic code and the reactivity system will automatically detect all changes without adding special tools or boilerplate.

2. **Effortlessly optimal** – data changes are tracked at runtime, which means the computations run only when needed and we avoid unnecessary component re-renders.

3. **Unopinionated** – **MobX** can be used with any UI framework, which makes your code decoupled, portable, and easily testable.

One more interesting concept in **MobX**-land is snapshots. If you have ever written tests for JavaScript applications, you may have heard the term "snapshot." **MobX** snapshots are similar to test snapshots. They save the state of the state tree at a given moment in time. Looking at **MobX** snapshots can be very handy during debugging or for making performant state updates after fetching data from the server. If you want to learn more about snapshots and debugging **MobX** states, I invite you to take a look at the `Egghead.io` course created by *Michel Westrate*, the creator of **MobX**; you can find the link in the *Further reading* section. As for fetching data from the server, we will look into that in this chapter, in the last section.

Now, we have a very theoretical hang on the main concepts of **MobX**. We know it's different from **Redux**, but you would probably like, my dear reader, to see some code! Let's move on to configuring **MobX** in the Funbook app.

Configuring MobX in the Funbook app

As promised by the **MobX** authors, the boilerplate for this library is minimal. We will have to add three dependencies and a couple of files for everything to work correctly. Let's start by adding the necessary dependencies by running the following command in the terminal:

```
npm install mobx mobx-state-tree –save
```

This command will install both **MobX** and **MobX**-State-Tree. **MobX** is unopinionated about the UI library we want to use it with. This means that when we decide to use a specific UI library, we will have to find a way to get it to cooperate with **MobX**. It so happens that we have chosen **React Native** as our UI library, so we need to add an additional dependency that will make **MobX** cooperate smoothly with React. Let's run the following command:

```
npm install mobx-react-lite –save
```

Now that we have our dependencies, let's run the following command:

```
expo start
```

It's a good idea to check frequently whether our app is still running correctly. Something as innocent as installing dependencies can sometimes break the app, and we want to know about any issues as soon as they arise.

Assuming everything is working as expected, we can move on to implementing **MobX** instead of **React**'s context in the Funbook app.

A little reminder, my dear reader, about the code: the code related to this chapter can be found in the `chapter-6` folder of this book's repository: `https://github.com/PacktPublishing/Simplifying-State-Management-in-React-Native/tree/main/chapter-6`. If you prefer to follow along on your own, please copy the `example-app-full` folder and start working from there.

Using MobX for FavoritedImages

At the beginning of this book, I made a choice, my dear reader, to write all examples in **JavaScript**. I have come to regret that decision while working on the examples with **MobX**. **MobX** documentation uses **TS**, a **JavaScript** superset, which brings many advantages. I encourage you my dear reader to learn about **TS**. I will not spend any more time on this topic as there are hundreds of hugely valuable TS resources both online and in book form, but I wanted to let you know, in case you read the **MobX** documentation, that the examples look a little different from the code in this book.

Now that we have all of this out of the way, let's get to coding! We will create a new folder called `models` where we will store data models for our app. The term "data models" may sound very serious to you, but don't worry. **MobX** data models are nothing more than **JavaScript** objects with superpowers – by which I mean to say, they look like simple **JavaScript** objects, but they are capable of doing much more!

When we have a couple of models ready, we will create one more file for our global **MobX**-managed state. We will call this file `store.js` and we will place all the logic for fetching and managing liked images in this file.

Let's start by creating the simplest model: for the user. We won't be implementing actual user state changes, but we'll just take a quick look at what **MobX** models look like in real-world implementation:

```
// ./models/User.js
import { types } from "mobx-state-tree"

export const User = types.model({
    name: types.string,
    loggedIn: types.boolean,
})
```

We only need to import one item: types from `mobx-state-tree`. These types are very powerful tools in **MobX**. You can declare very simple types, such as the ones here – a string and a Boolean – but you can also declare that these values are optional, as follows:

```
name: types.optional(types.string, "")
```

You can also tell **MobX** what the default values are (that's what the `""` symbols after the `types.string` definition in the preceding example signify), or that a given value may be undefined, like so:

```
name: types.maybe(types.string)
```

There are many more types out there, but we won't be covering all of them. However, the MST documentation has a very thorough section on types, and you can find a link to this in the *Further reading* section.

You may have noticed that `types.model` is also at the very beginning of the declaration. This is what indicates to **MobX** that we are describing the shape of our data.

Our `Users` model is very simple. We used it to get a first glance at **MobX** data models. Now, it's time to dig into something more interesting: the `LikedImages` model.

We start again by importing `types` from `mobx-state-tree` and declaring the shape of a single `LikedImage` item:

```
// ./models/LikedImages
import { types } from "mobx-state-tree"

const LikedImageItem = types
    .model({
        itemId: types.number,
        authorId: types.number,
        timeStamp: types.string,
        url: types.string,
        likes: types.string,
        conversations: types.string,
    })
```

We added a few properties to the `LikedImageItem` model. We will use those properties in the future to display the necessary data on the `Favorited` surface. It just so happens that these properties are present in the image items fetched from the server.

Now that the single image model has been described, we can move on to setting up the array of identical images and the actions related to this array:

```
export const LikedImages = types
    .model({
        imageList: types.optional
            (types.array(LikedImageItem), []),
    })
    .actions(self => ({
        addLikedImage(newImage) {
            // will add images here
        },
        removeLikedImage(imageToRemove) {
            // will remove images here
        },

    }))
```

Starting from the top, you will notice that we are declaring an object called `imageList`, which will store an array of `LikedImageItems`, and will be instantiated with the default value of an empty array.

The `LikedImageItem` model doesn't do anything interesting, so let's move on to the `LikedImages` array. We have to add a `types.model`, where we tell our state manager that this piece of state will be an array of `LikedImageItems` – and then we add placeholders for the two functions that need to be created: adding and removing liked images.

We can now continue setting up **MobX** in our app. First of all, we will set up a store – similarly to **Redux**-managed apps, this will be the source of truth for the app. We will then fetch data from the server and pass it to the app. Once we have all of that ready, we will look at **MobX** actions – events to which our models will need to respond. Last, but not least, we'll learn about deriving data from the state.

Creating the store

Before adding and removing images, there's one more step we need to take. What do you think, my dear reader? Yes, we need to hook up the store!

Let's go to our `store.js` file and tell it to use the `User` and `LikedImages` models. We'll start by importing all the necessary files and creating an empty store:

```
import { types, flow, applySnapshot } from "mobx-state-tree"
import { LikedImages } from "./src/models/LikedImages";
import { User } from './src/models/User';
```

```
const RootStore = types
    .model({
        users: User,
        likedImages: LikedImages
    })

export const store = RootStore.create({
    users: {},
    likedImages: {}
})
```

As you may remember, my dear reader, **MobX** and **MST** are unopinionated as far as the UI is concerned. This means we need to look for detailed instructions on how to best integrate **MST** with our **React Native** app. It just so happens that the documentation recommends using **React**'s context to share trees between components. Our example is small so far and we will concentrate on one tree (the favorited images); however, it's good to get set up correctly for our app to scale. And also: we understand context very well from the previous chapters, right? So, this is going to be a piece of cake:

```
const RootStoreContext = React.createContext(null);

export const Provider = RootStoreContext.Provider;

export function useMst() {
    const store = useContext(RootStoreContext);

  if (store === null) {
      throw new Error("Store cannot be null,
        please add a context provider");
  }
  return store;
}
```

In the preceding code, we are creating a very simple context, which will be the vessel for **MobX** state. We also added a useMst hook (as in, "use **MobX-State-Tree**") to consume data from the **React** context. We also added a handy error message in case anything goes wrong. We start with a context with a value of null and we will pass the real store when we add the <Provider> to our app:

```
// App.js
//...
Import { Provider, store } from "./store.js"

//...
export default function App() {
//...
  return (
    <SafeAreaProvider>
      //...
          <Provider value={store}>
```

Remember to wrap your app in the `Provider` created for the **MobX** state. This is what is shown in the preceding code snippet.

Now that we've declared the store and our models, wrapped the app in a `Provider`, and passed the store to this `Provider`, we need to pull in the data from **MobX** in the component. Let's go to `ListOfFavorited.js` and replace the pure **React** context used previously with **MobX** data:

```
import { useMst } from '../../store';

export const ListOfFavorites = ({ navigation }) => {
  const { likedImages } = useMst();
  //...
  return (
    //...
    >
      <FlatList
        data={likedImages.imageList}
        //...
```

This is going pretty nicely, don't you think? We have our `ListOfFavoritedImages` component ready! Yes? Let's check in the app:

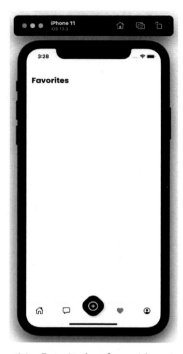

Figure 6.1 – Favorited surface with no images

All we see is a blank screen on the **Favorited** surface. What happened? We forgot to fetch the images! Let's see how to do that in the next section.

Fetching data

We have our image list stored on the server. **MobX-State-Tree** proposes two ways of fetching asynchronous data, but both are actions. Let's create an action in the store:

```
// ./store.js
const RootStore = types
    .model({
        users: User,
        likedImages: LikedImages
    })
    .actions(self => ({
```

```
        async fetchImages() {
                const response = await fetch(requestBase + "/
                    john_doe/likedImages.json");
                const data = await response.json();
                return data;
        }
    }))
```

We need an asynchronous function that will do the fetching – we have called it fetchImages. This function uses JavaScript's fetch function and returns data from the server. Now that we have the data, we need to pass it into the LikedImages model. Let's add a function that will do just that:

```
// ./store.js
const RootStore = types
    //…
    .actions(self => ({
        setLikedImages(newImages) {
            store.likedImages.imageList.replace(newImages)
        },
        async fetchImages() {
                const response = await fetch(requestBase + "/
                    john_doe/likedImages.json");
                const data = await response.json();
                store.setLikedImages(data);
        }
    }))
```

The newly added setLikedImages function takes care of replacing the entire array of images with anything that's passed to it. We also adjusted the fetchImages function, to pass the result of the fetch into setLikedImages.

Now that we have told our app where to get the data from and where to put it, we only need to add WHEN. We could call the store.fetchImages() function directly from the app when it's rendered. However, there is a more elegant solution: using the life cycle hooks provided by **MobX**. One of those hooks is called afterCreate, and it's called, as you may expect, after a given store is created. Let's add this hook to the list of actions in our store:

```
// ./store.js
const RootStore = types
    //…
```

```
    .actions(self => ({
        afterCreate() {
            self.fetchImages();
        },
        //...
    }))
```

Ta-da! Our app will know what to fetch (the data from the server), where to put it once it's fetched (in the `LikedImages` array), and when to do so (when the store is created). If you check the app now, you should see the list of images rendered correctly.

The code we wrote works fine, but we can improve it further. **MobX** and **MST** offer us optimized solutions for writing async logic. Their solution is called generator functions. This may sound scary at first, but don't worry. All we need to do is import a couple of utilities from MST and change the syntax of our function slightly:

```
// ./store.js
  import { types, flow, applySnapshot } from "mobx-state-tree"


//...
    .actions(self => ({
        afterCreate() {
            self.fetchImages();
        },
        fetchImages: flow(function* fetchImages() {
            const response = yield fetch(requestBase + "/
                john_doe/likedImages.json");
            applySnapshot(self.likedImages.imageList,
                yield response.json());
        })
```

The `fetchImages` function in this version uses a generator. For **MobX** to understand that this is a generator, we wrap it with `flow` and use * with the `function` keyword. Then, we replace `async/await` with `yield`, which pauses the function and returns a `Promise`.

As you may have noticed, we removed the `setLikedImages` action in this version of the code. It is not needed anymore, as we're using another **MST** utility called `applySnapshot`. I've mentioned briefly before what snapshots in **MobX** are: they are **JavaScript** objects representing the state tree at any given moment. Using the `applySnapshot` utility here, we are making sure the update is optimized, as only the necessary data is updated.

This version of the code produces the same result as the previous one. However, it is written in fewer lines of code and uses practices recommended by the authors of **MobX**. It's a good idea to write code in the recommended way – it helps us avoid bugs and performance issues. We surely know less about **MobX** than its author and maintainers, so let's follow their lead.

Okay – we're making great progress here. We have the data models and we have wired them up into a store. We passed the store into our app thanks to a `Provider`, and we fetched the initial data. The only thing left is to add actions and make this app come alive!

Adding actions

Let's go back to our `LikedImages` model and add some real code for the `addImages` action:

```
.actions(self => ({
        addLikedImage(newImage) {
            self.imageList.unshift(newImage)
        },
```

The `actions` function itself holds a reference to the entire array of liked images – this is the `self` keyword. In the first iteration of the **MobX** library, you could find uses of a known **JavaScript** keyword: `this`. `this` can unfortunately be confusing for many developers, which is why **MobX** introduced `self`. Plus, **MobX** realizes that if you're doing an action on a model, you probably need access to that model, so it serves us what we need!

Now that we have a reference to the `LikedImages` array, we want to add a new item to that array. We could use `.push()`, but I chose to use `.unshift()`, which will push the new item to the top of the array and effectively display it at the top of the list of images on the `Favorites` surface.

The place where we would like to call this action is `ImageDetailsModal`, because we can "like" images from within this modal. This modal has a heart button. When it's tapped, we would like the image to be added to our user's array of liked images:

```
// ./surfaces/ImageDetailsModal.js
export const ImageDetailsModal = ({ navigation, route }) => {
  const { likedImages } = useMst();

//...
<Pressable
        onPress={() => {
            likedImages.addLikedImage(route.params.imageItem)
        }}
    >
```

Beautiful! Now, when we tap this pressable heart icon on an image from the main feed, we should see the image added on the Favorited surface, right? Unfortunately, not yet. **MobX** doesn't have a lot of boilerplate, but we do need to tell it what data to observe. We have to add an `observer` wrapper to the `ListOfFavorited` component. This `observer` wrapper will re-render our component when it detects a change in the data models:

```
// ./components/ListOfFavorited
import { useMst } from '../../store';
import { observer } from "mobx-react-lite"

export const ListOfFavorites = observer(({ navigation }) => {
  const { likedImages } = useMst();
```

And now we're almost done! There's only one small catch left. When you like an image and then go back to the Favorited surface, you probably won't see the new image until you start scrolling. This is not the functionality we're looking for. We would like to see the newly liked image appear immediately. The issue here is **React Native's** `FlatList` component, which accepts simple arrays, but we're trying to pass a special sort of array from our **MobX** model: an observable array.

> **Making FlatList play nice with MobX**
> In order for our `FlatList` to render the updated data correctly, we need to use the `values` utility provided by MobX.

Here's the code of `FlatList` in the `ListOfFavorited` component:

```
Import { values } from "mobx"

<FlatList
        data={values(likedImages.imageList)}
```

`Values` is a collection utility provided by the MST library that returns all values in the collection as an array, which is exactly what `FlatList` is expecting. You can read more about collection utilities in **MobX** in their documentation, and you can find a link in the *Further reading* section.

Now, everything should be working as expected. Make sure to check your phone or phone simulator frequently. The sooner you discover errors and issues, the easier they are to debug.

Deriving data from state

I've mentioned the fact that **MobX's** authors state that anything that can be derived from state should be. We'll get a chance to derive some data now.

We would like to know which images are liked and which are not so that we can successfully add them to the list of liked images or avoid duplicating them. Deriving data from the state is done on the data models through `views`. I've decided to add this following view to the store because we are working in a constrained environment, and I want to keep things simple. Here's the **view** that I have added to the `RootStore` model:

```
const RootStore = types
//…
    .views(self => ({
        getIsImageLiked(itemId) {
            return values(self.likedImages?.imageList).filter(
                (favoritedImg) => favoritedImg.itemId ===
                    itemId
            ).length > 0;
        }
    }))
```

As with `actions`, you will notice the `self` keyword here. It holds a reference to the current data model for easy access.

I created a `getIsImageLiked` function by passing it an image ID. We then filter over the entire liked images array to check whether that image ID exists.

Sure, this is not the most efficient way to check a user's liked images in a social media app, which could potentially be hundreds upon hundreds of images – but we do want to see what these views are about, and this is a great chance to do so.

Let's go back to `ImageDetailsModal`, where we would like to check whether a given image is liked or not and then display the appropriate icon (an empty heart for images that are not liked and a filled-in heart for liked images) and pass the appropriate function (either adding or removing it from the liked images array).

If you copied your code from the `example-app-full` folder, you'll find `useEffect` in this component, which takes care of checking this exact thing. Let's try simply replacing the old React context values with the new values from the **MobX** store. Does the code work? Go ahead and check, I'll be waiting right here.

Something is not quite right, right? The code does not work as expected. To be honest, it does not work at all. If you tried to work out step by step what was happening, and what should be happening between **MobX** tree updates and **React's** `useEffect` changes, you may have found that it's not that simple to figure out. The precedence of side effects can be very complicated, and it gets even more complicated in bigger apps – and that is why we use **MobX's** dedicated tools: views.

Going back to our code, we can go ahead and remove `useEffect` completely. We're taking care of the filtering in `views`, which is added to the store. Let's use `import` from the context hook and use the values provided by **MobX**:

```
export const ImageDetailsModal = observer(({ navigation,
  route }) => {
const { likedImages, getIsImageLiked } = useMst();
  const isCurrentImageLiked = getIsImageLiked
    (route.params.imageItem.itemId)
```

Don't forget to add the `observer` wrapper for our component to observe changes in data!

The heart icon is working as expected now – it looks filled in when an image has been liked on the `Favorited` surface and gets filled in when an un-liked image is newly liked.

We have gone over creating data models and setting up the store, actions, and views in our **MobX**-managed version of the Funbook app. By now, we have an app with **MobX** and **MobX-State-Tree** as state managers. We're fetching and mutating data; we are even deriving data from our state! There is still a lot to do in order to convert all of the states and functionalities of the app to **MobX**. Feel free to play around on your own, or check out the `chapter-6-complete` folder if you would just like to see the complete app.

Summary

We have just gone over the main ideas and the implementation of **MobX** and **MobX-State-Tree** in the Funbook app. **MobX** may not be as popular as **Redux** in the **React** ecosystem, but it does hold a very important place, nonetheless. **MobX** presents a different way of looking at the state than Redux does and a very different way of managing it. We created data models and attached actions to them. If you are a developer trying to understand an existing app for the first time, having the data and actions in one place may be very helpful to understand what is going on more quickly. **MobX** takes this state centralization one step further by introducing views. We have all the tools necessary for creating and managing a state accessibly from the very same place where we declare the shape of the state. The last step is to add `observer` wrappers to the components that need to be aware of state changes and then we have a very nice **MobX**-managed app.

It's great to know how you can manage states in a **React Native** app. It's even better to know a few different ways to do so – and if you like different options, you'll be happy to know that we will talk about **XState** in the next chapter!

Further reading

- `https://mobx.js.org/README.html`: MobX documentation.

- `https://mobx-state-tree.js.org/intro/welcome`: MobX-State-Tree.

- `https://egghead.io/courses/manage-application-state-with-mobx-state-tree`: *Manage Application State with Mobx-state-tree.*

- `https://www.packtpub.com/product/mobx-quick-start-guide/9781789344837`: *MobX Quick Start Guide.*

- `https://github.com/infinitered/ignite`: Ignite – React Native boilerplate by Infinite Red.

- `https://reactnativeradio.com/episodes/rnr-241-redux-toolkit-vs-mobx-state-tree-showdown`: Redux Toolkit versus MobX-State-Tree.

- `https://www.loom.com/share/9e3afe0547824e42bada06191e891ae1`: *Intro to MobX-State-Tree and MobX-React* by *Jamon Holmgren.*

- `https://mobx-state-tree.js.org/overview/types`: MST types.

- `https://mobx.js.org/collection-utilities.html`: MobX collection utilities.

7
Untangling Complex Flows in React Native Apps with XState

In the previous chapter, we took a look at **MobX**—the second most popular state management library in the **React** ecosystem. MobX introduced some new concepts, such as using state values derived by the state manager. Other high-level concepts were similar to **Redux**—such as presenting state as plain **JavaScript** objects. We will now look at the first outlier on the React-state-management horizon: **XState**. XState treats the state not as an object, but as a finite machine. Don't worry if you haven't heard that term yet, as we'll go over the topic of finite machines in the first section of this chapter.

We will start by looking at the theoretical side of XState's basic idea: state machines. We will then talk about other high-level concepts of XState—state charts, actions, and the XState visualizer. When we're comfortable with the theory, we'll configure XState in the Funbook app, and then we will implement XState for managing liking images in the app.

Here's a complete list of what is covered in this chapter:

- What are finite state machines?
- What is XState—high-level concepts
- Configuring XState in the Funbook app
- Using XState for the `FavoritedImages` surface

By the end of this chapter, you will be able to understand and use XState as the state management solution for your projects. You will understand what a state machine is and how it differs from state objects used in other state management libraries. I hope that you will also start seeing which solutions you prefer using.

Technical requirements

In order to follow along with this chapter, you will need some knowledge of JavaScript and **ReactJS**. If you have followed at least *Chapters 1* through *4* of this book, you should be able to go forward without any issues.

Feel free to use an IDE of your choice, as React Native does not need any specific functionality. Currently, the most popular IDEs for frontend developers are Microsoft's VS Code, Atom, Sublime Text, and WebStorm.

The code snippets provided in this chapter are here to illustrate what we should be doing with the code—they do not provide the whole picture. For a better experience of coding along, please open the GitHub repo in your IDE and look at the files in there. You can start with the files in either the folder named `example-app-full` or `chapter-7`. If you start with `example-app-full`, you will be responsible for implementing the solutions described in this chapter. If you choose to look at `chapter-7` you will see the entire solution implemented by me.

If you get stuck or lost, you can check the code in the GitHub repo:

`https://github.com/PacktPublishing/Simplifying-State-Management-in-React-Native/tree/main/chapter-7`.

What are finite state machines?

If I were to ask you, my dear reader, to guess what finite state machines are, you would probably say they are related to managing state in applications. After all, this whole book is on that topic!

Funny thing is, finite state machines have nothing to do with applications; they have nothing to do with React or even programming at all. A finite state machine is a mathematical model of computation. It's an abstract concept that can be applied to real-life objects or problems, and it represents a machine that can be in exactly one of a finite number of states at any given time. The predefined states can be changed from one to another in response to some user input. Traffic lights are an example of a simple finite state machine: a traffic light can be green, red, or yellow at any time, and it should never display two colors at once. Another example of a simple state machine is an elevator. The default state of an elevator is to stand still with doors closed. When a user pushes the button summoning the elevator, the elevator transitions to a state of movement. When it reaches the right floor, it opens and closes the doors. The elevator then goes back to the default, idle state, waiting for the next user input.

If you wish to find out more about this theoretical concept, you will find a link to a very thorough *Wikipedia* page on finite state machines in the *Further reading* section. As for this book, it's time to find out why we are talking about this concept at all. Can you guess? I bet you can! Finite state machines are the basic concept of the state management library we're analyzing in this chapter: XState.

What is XState – high-level concepts

Now that we have a grasp on the theoretical concept of finite state machines, we can move on to talking about XState and its main concept: finite state machines! But this time, we'll look at it in the world of programming global state in applications.

When using XState to manage global state in an application, we should think of our state as a finite state machine. This means abandoning the previous concept of representing state as a plain JavaScript object. With XState, a component—or a surface—is a machine that can be in one of multiple predefined states. Let's consider the user login flow. Our entire app can be in one of two states: the user is logged in or the user is not logged in. We would also need a transition mechanism for the user to move from one of the states to the other. The same goes for images on the **Home** surface. Every image is either in the state of being "liked" or "not liked". The user can change the current state of the image by clicking the heart icon below the image.

Besides finite state machines, there are two other important concepts used in XState: **statecharts** and the **actor model**. Statecharts are basically drawings that can be used to represent state machines. Here's an example of a statechart representing the state and transitions of a light bulb:

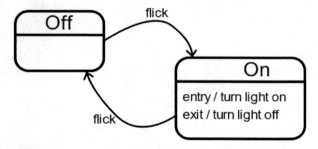

Figure 7.1 – Simple statechart drawing of a light switch

The preceding diagram serves as a very simple state machine. When working on a mobile application, you may find yourself working on much more complicated state machines. Starting from something as trivial as a form, you can find yourself adding multiple states, such as enabled/disabled, valid/invalid, and clean/dirty, on multiple elements. Without statecharts, you would face a state explosion. As fun as it may sound, it's not great to face in an app. Let's take a look at the example of complex inputs drawn out with state transitions:

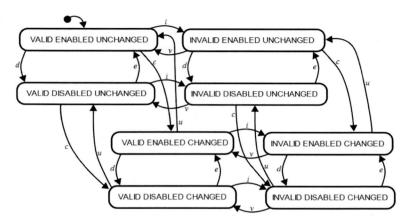

Figure 7.2 – Complex state chart

The user clicks on a valid input and enters the **Valid Enabled Unchanged** state. The app transitions automatically into an **Invalid Enabled Unchanged** state. When the user provides some input, the app will be in an **Invalid Enabled Changed** state. If the input provided by the user is valid, we will land in a **Valid Enabled Changed** state; if not, we will return to **Invalid Enabled Changed**. What if the user clicks something else in the form—let's say, a radio box that disables the first input? We go into an **Invalid** (or **Valid**) **Disabled Changed** state. It's rather hard to reason about this chart. This is the moment when statechart features come into play. Statecharts offer an implementation of parallel states, hierarchies, and guards. You can read more on those concepts in this document recommended in the XState documentation: `https://statecharts.dev/state-machine-state-explosion.html`.

The last big idea behind XState is actor models. This is a mathematical model of computation, stating that everything is an "actor" and can do three things: receive messages, send messages, and do something with the received messages.

I was very lucky to be able to ask XState's author, *David Khourshid*, a few questions on the topic of his state management library. He told me he "*created XState for two reasons: to manage complex logic and to visualize complex logic. State machines and statecharts are visual formalisms that excel in representing even the most complex flows and logic in a visually clear way, and I wanted a simple way to use them in JavaScript applications.*" He added that the high-level ideas of XState were heavily influenced by the **World Wide Web Consortium (W3C) State Chart XML (SCXML)** specification.

Let's take a quick detour to find out what SCXML is and what it means that it has a W3C specification. Depending on your experience in programming, you may have heard of the **Extensible Markup Language (XML)** file format and markup language. XML is used to store, transmit, and reconstruct data. XML files are easy to read when properly indented and formatted, as they simply describe data.

SCXML is a cousin of XML. It's an XML-based markup language used for providing a state-machine-based environment. The fact that it has a W3C specification means that it can be used for various internet-related programs with great confidence. You can find a link to the entire W3C specification in the *Further reading* section.

Going back to XState, not only has it been influenced by SCXML, but it is also fully compatible with it, which means you could write an SCXML document describing states, and it will work with an XState implementation in your React Native app. You can also write it in JavaScript. Whatever rocks your boat!

I asked David Khourshid about the future of his library. XState is an open source project, as with all the other state management libraries we talk about in this book. David said maintaining XState and working on XState-related tools is his full-time job. He is working on new and powerful collaborative editing tools for the XState visualizer. He said: *"the next major version of XState (version 5) will have many more features, be more modular, and have "actors" as first-class citizens. Actors are entities that can send and receive messages, and state machines are just one of many behaviors that an actor can have. You can also represent actors as promises, observables, reducers, and more, which will allow developers to use XState's API (and visual tools) for all of their logic, not just the state-machine-specific logic."*

You may have noticed a mention of an XState visualizer in the previous paragraph. This tool is something that absolutely sets XState apart from other state management libraries. Thanks to this visualizer, you can see a graphical representation of states and transitions between states in your app. You can use it to plan a new app or debug an app that you are working on. You can find the visualizer at `https://xstate.js.org/viz/`. Here's an example screenshot of what it looks like:

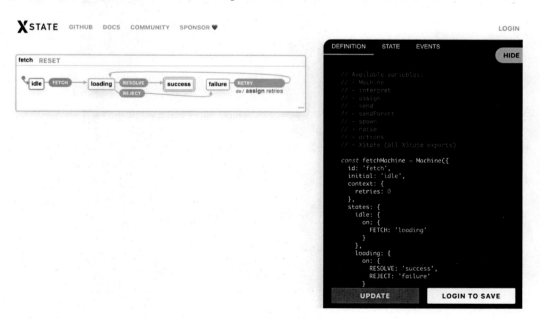

Figure 7.3 – Screenshot of the XState visualizer

David said that the visualizer is one of the hardest things he has worked on. It's always a work in progress, and it has gone through many iterations. Currently, it's an *SVG-based 'canvas' with HTML inside."* Even though it's somewhat interactive right now—you can click on transitions and observe how the state changes—David said that *"making it interactive is yet another layer of difficulty, especially for drag-and-drop interactions and modifying the statechart."* Personally, I'm very excited about the new versions of the visualizer. It has helped me many times to plan the best possible state machine for the apps I worked on (that used XState).

In this section, we have talked about the main ideas behind XState. They are different from all the previous approaches we analyzed. The entire library is based on the mathematical concept of finite state machines. It also uses the theories behind statecharts and actor models, to make sure managing state in a complex app can be done effectively. Now, it's time to see this library in action. Let's move on to implementing XState in the Funbook app.

Configuring XState in the Funbook app

Let's see what it takes to use XState in a real app. If you would like to follow along on your own, you can copy the `example-app-full` folder and use it as a starting point. If you prefer to look at the code related to this chapter, please look in the `chapter-7` folder: `https://github.com/PacktPublishing/Simplifying-State-Management-in-React-Native/tree/main/chapter-7`.

First things first—we need to add XState to the project. You can do so by running one of the two following commands:

```
npm install xstate@latest --save
// or
yarn add xstate@latest --save
```

XState itself is an unopinionated library, much like MobX. This means it is not ready out-of-the-box to work with React. The XState documentation has a section called *Recipes* where you can read more on the implementation with React or other UI libraries, such as Vue or Svelte. As for us, we need to add the React-related dependency, `xstate-react`. Let's do this by running one of the two following commands:

```
npm install xstate-react@latest --save
// or
yarn add xstate-react@latest --save
```

Now that we have the dependencies ready, let's run the app to make sure everything is working as expected. If everything is OK, we can create our very first state machine. We will start with a simple example: user login flow. At a high level, there isn't much logic involved in this flow. The user can be either logged in or out, and they transition from one state to the other and back:

```
import { createMachine } from 'xstate';

export const userFlowMachine = createMachine({
  id: 'userFlow',
  initial: 'anonymous',
  states: {
    anonymous,
    authenticated,
  }
});
```

Reading through the code is rather logical. We start by importing a createMachine function, which we call to create our userFlowMachine instance. In userFlowMachine, we start by defining the machine ID and the initial state. We then continue to define the two possible states of the app. The user in our app can be anonymous or authenticated. But how can the user transition from one state to the other? Let's add this functionality to the state machine:

```
import { createMachine } from 'xstate';

export const userFlowMachine = createMachine({
  id: 'userFlow',
  initial: 'anonymous',
  states: {
    anonymous: {
      on: {
        LOGIN: { target: 'authenticated' },
      }
    },
    authenticated: {
        on: {
            LOGOUT: { target: 'anonymous' },
          }
```

```
        },
    }
});
```

Great! Now, the user can be in the anonymous state, from which they can transition using the LOGIN transition. At this moment, they will be in the authenticated state, from which they can transition using the LOGOUT transition. You could continue improving this example by adding some implementation details to the LOGIN and LOGOUT transitions, or maybe an error state. But I will stop talking about this particular state machine now and see how it should be used in a React app.

Unsurprisingly, the XState docs recommend using React Context to manage global state with XState. Luckily for us, we have a good handle on React Context by now, right? So, let's look at an example of React Context in the XState documentation:

```
import React, { createContext } from 'react';
import { useInterpret } from '@xstate/react';
import { userFlowMachine } from './machines/userFlowMachine';

export const GlobalStateContext = createContext({});

export const GlobalStateProvider = (props) => {
  const userFlowService = useInterpret(userFlowMachine);

  return (
    <GlobalStateContext.Provider value={{ userFlowService }}>
      {props.children}
    </GlobalStateContext.Provider>
  );
};
```

Hmm… what is this useInterpret() function? It's imported from xstate-react, and it's a special tool to make sure we don't cause too many re-renders when using React Context. useInterpret() returns a service, which is a reference to the state machine. As per the XState documentation: "*this value never changes, so we don't need to worry about wasted re-renders.*"

> **Knowing your tools**
> Every tool was created with an idea of how it should be used. You could take a hammer and use the wooden handle to hit a nail, but you have learned this is not how hammers work best. The same rule applies to JavaScript libraries. No one was born with the knowledge of JavaScript libraries and tooling. We all must read the documentation and learn our tools' best practices.

We have a way to create context, so now, let's go through XState's instructions for using it. We will have to subscribe to the service of the global context we defined at the root of the app. Here's what such a subscription would look like:

```
import React, { useContext } from 'react';
import { GlobalStateContext } from './globalState';
import { useActor } from '@xstate/react';

export const SomeComponent = (props) => {
  const globalServices = useContext(GlobalStateContext);
  const [state] = useActor(globalServices. userFlowService);

    return state.matches('loggedIn') ? 'Logged In' :
      'Logged Out';
};
```

We have completed the basic setup for XState in a React Native app. There are many paths to be taken now: improving performance, dispatching events, or using state selectors. We will go over the necessary steps in the next section, where we will set up XState for the `LikedImages` surface and the modal responsible for adding liked images.

Using XState for the FavoritedImages surface

In the previous section, we set up a basic machine that could be used to control the user flow in the app. Let's add a new machine, for our real-world use case: liking images in a social media clone app.

We'll start by creating a machine **minimum viable product** (**MVP**):

```
// src/machines/likeImagesMachine.js
import { createMachine } from "xstate";

export const likeImagesMachine = createMachine({
  id: "likeImagesMachine",
  context: {
    likedImages: [
        { Example Image Object 1},
        { Example Image Object 2}
        ...
        ],
```

```
  },
  initial: "loading",
  states: {
    loading: {},
    ready: {},
    error: {},
  },
});
```

Let's analyze this code from the top: we start by importing the `createMachine` function, which we use on the very first line of the `likeImagesMachine` function. We set the ID of the machine and the context. Bear in mind that XState context is different from React context. We've talked a lot about ReactJS context; we know it can be used to share state between components. XState context is a container for quantitative data (such as strings, arrays, or objects), which can potentially be infinite. The array of liked images is a great example of this sort of data, and that's why we'll be keeping this array in our machine's context. For testing purposes, we will add a couple of images to this default array of `likedImages` in the context. All that's left is defining states of our machine and setting the default state. Easy-peasy!

We will start by creating and configuring a wrapper for the state, with the help of React's context. Once everything is set up correctly with mock data, we will fetch real data from our backend. Having fetched data, we will write the last piece of code: managing liked images with XState.

Configuring context and components

Now is the time to talk about the first type of context: React context. We set up a nifty context with the user flow in the previous section. We will add the liked images machine to this context:

```
// src/context.js
[…]
import { useInterpret } from "@xstate/react";
  import { likeImagesMachine } from "./machines/
    likeImagesMachine ";
import { userFlow } from "./machines/userFlowMachine";

export const GlobalStateContext = createContext({});

export const useXStateContext = () => {
  const context = React.useContext(GlobalStateContext);
  if (context === undefined) {
```

```
      throw new Error(
          " useXStateContext must be used within a
          GlobalStateContextProvider"
      );
  }
  return context;
};

export const GlobalStateProvider = (props) => {
  const likedImagesAppService =
useInterpret(likeImagesMachine);
  const userFlowService = useInterpret(userFlow);

  const mergedServices = {
    likedImagesAppService,
    userFlowService,
  };

  return (
    <GlobalStateContext.Provider value={mergedServices}>
      {props.children}
    </GlobalStateContext.Provider>
  );
};
```

This is a good moment to improve the basic context we set up in the previous, more theoretical part of this chapter. We will do so by adding a new custom hook called useXStateContext. Using custom hooks with React context is a best practice that we covered in previous chapters. In the GlobalStateProvider function, we added likedImagesMachine through the useInterpret custom hook provided by the good people at XState. We merge the interpreted machines and pass them as the context value. The last piece of the context value is wrapping the component in context. We will have to keep the global state at the very root of the app so that both the FavoritedImages surface and ImageDetailsModal can reach it. Here's what your App.js should roughly look like:

```
// src/App.js
[...]
import {
  [...]
```

```
        GlobalStateProvider
          } from "./src/context";

[...]

return (
    <SafeAreaProvider>
      <GlobalStateProvider>
        <UserStateContext.Provider value={userLoggedIn}>
[...]
```

Let's use this brand-new machine, interpreted by React context and holding a few example images in its own context, in the FavoritedImages surface. The list of favorited images is rendered in the ListOfFavorites component, and this is the component we will be changing:

```
// src/components/ListOfFavorties.js
import { useXStateContext } from "../context";
import { useActor } from "@xstate/react";

export const ListOfFavorites = ({ navigation }) => {
  const globalServices = useXStateContext();
    const [state] = useActor(globalServices.
      likedImagesAppService);
    const [imageData, updateImageData] = useState
      (state.context.likedImages);

//...
  return (
    //...
      <FlatList
        data={imageData}
//...
```

We start by importing the custom useXStateContext hook we created to easily consume React context. The second thing we need to import is XState's useActor hook. This is a React hook that subscribes to emitted changes from a given interpreted state machine, named by the XState author "an actor." If you go to the XState documentation, you will find there are other implementations of the useActor function, tailored for use with Svelte, Vue, and other libraries. This is because XState, much like MobX, is unopinionated when it comes to UI libraries.

Finally, we need to use all those imported items in our component. We pull in data from React context, and we subscribe to changes through the `useActor` hook. We could use the state returned from the `useActor` hook directly. However, React Native's `FlatList` needs to be informed of data changes very clearly to update. Therefore, I added a `useState` hook, including the `updateImageData` setter function, which will come in handy once we try to add images to this array dynamically.

Speaking of dynamically, it's time to think about data fetching through XState. But before we go any further, make sure to run your app with the current changes and make sure you can see the example images from the `likeImagesMachine` function on the `FavoritedImages` surface. If you do encounter any errors, you can look at your terminal window, as many XState errors will be described there. They should also be visible on your phone simulator or physical device. Here's an example error you may see in the console and in the simulator at the same time:

Figure 7.4 – XState errors in the console and phone simulator

Fetching image data

Fetching data isn't always the strong suit of state management libraries. After all, it's not their basic responsibility. In the case of XState, however, fetching comes very naturally as every Promise can be modeled as a state machine. At a high level, we need to kick off a function that will be in a default "loading" state. We'll wait for something to happen with it—either resolve or reject—and go to the appropriate "resolved" or "rejected" states. Here's how our image-fetching machine is shaping up:

```js
// src/machines/fetchMachine.js
import { createMachine, assign } from "xstate";

export const fetchImagesMachine = createMachine({
  id: "fetchImages",
  initial: "loading",
  context: {
    retries: 0,
    images: [],
  },
  states: {
    loading: {
      on: {
        RESOLVE: "success",
        REJECT: "failure",
      },
    },
    success: {
      type: "final",
    },
    failure: {
      on: {
        RETRY: {
          target: "loading",
          actions: assign({
            retries: (context, event) => context.retries+1,
          }),
        },
      },
    },
```

```
      },
    },
});
```

What you can see here is a very simple machine, prepared to describe the process of fetching data from an external source. We have three states: the initial state of `loading`, and `success` and `failure` states. You can see two actions in the `loading` state, which could be used to manage the fetching mechanism. There's also a `retry` action in the `failure` state. We could use it in the app to let the users manually try to fetch data when an error occurs. As far as the basic setup is concerned, this is all good, but we need to see how to call a real endpoint. In order to do so, we will change the `loading` state:

```
//...
states: {
    loading: {
      invoke: {
        id: 'fetchImagesFunction',
        src: async () => {
          const response = await fetch(
            requestBase + "/john_doe/likedImages.json"
          );
          const imageData = await response.json();
          return imageData;
        },
        onDone: {
          target: "success",
          actions: assign((context, event) => {
            return {
              images: event.data,
            };
          }),
        },
        onError: {
          target: "failure",
          actions: assign({
              error: (context, event) => "Oops!
                Something went wrong",
          }),
```

```
        },
      },
    },
```

Instead of two actions that could be called manually, I added the `invoke` property to the `loading` state. This way, the images will be loaded automatically when the machine is spawned, without needing user interaction. The `invoke` property's value is an object that contains the `id` and `src` properties of the function that is to be invoked. It is possible to invoke Promises, callbacks—which can send and receive events from the parent machine—observables—which can send events to the parent machine—and entire machines. We will stay on the simple side of things, and we will add an async `fetch` function to the source. You may also create a named function anywhere outside of the machine and invoke it through `src`. We are also using two optional values from the `invoke` property: `onDone` and `onError`. These two transitions come in handy when handling Promises. They act like any other XState transition—they include actions and the target state. Both actions include the `assign` keyword. `assign` is a function that updates the machine's context. We use it here to pass the resulting fetched data to the context so that we can use it later in our app. Assigner functions have some caveats: they have to be pure, and they surrender to a strict order. If you want to read more about them, please check the links provided in the *Further reading* section.

If everything works fine, you should be able to fetch images thanks to this function. But how do we use those images in the `likeImagesMachine` function? Remember that `invoke` property we just used for the Promise? We'll use that same property on `likeImagesMachine` in the loading state, to invoke this fetching machine and pass the fetched data thanks to the `onDone` function:

```
// src/machines/likeImagesMachine.js
import { fetchImagesMachine } from "./fetchImagesMachine";

export const likeImagesMachine = createMachine({
  id: "likeImagesMachine ",
  context: {
    likedImages: [],
    currentImage: null,
  },
  initial: "loading",
  states: {
    loading: {
      invoke: {
        id: "fetchImagesMachine",
        src: fetchImagesMachine,
        onDone: {
```

```
          target: "ready",
          actions: assign({
            likedImages: (context, event) => {
              return event.data.images;
            },
          }),
        },
      },
    },
//...
```

In this code snippet, we've imported the `fetchImagesMachine` function and we invoke it in the loading state of the `likeImagesMachine` function. Let's take a closer look at the assigner function we're using to pass image data from `fetchImagesMachine` to this parent machine. It has an onDone function, which will be called when `fetchImagesMachine` reaches its final state. This function assigns data returned from the invoked machine to the `context` of `likeImagesMachine`, and the data is passed through `event`. You will notice we're calling `event.data.images`. Where did that come from? This is something we need to add to `fetchImagesMachine`. So far, that machine only passed fetched data to its `context`, but we need to expose it so that the parent machine, `likeImagesMachine`, can access it. We already know the onDone event in the parent (`likeImagesMachine`) is called when the child (`fetchImagesMachine`) reaches its final state. The final state in our case is `success`. This is where we can add the `data` property:

```
// src/machines/fetchImagesMachine.js
//...
success: {
      type: "final",
      data: {
        images: (context, event) => context.images,
      },
    },
//...
```

This block of code tells the `fetchImagesMachine` function to add a `data` object to its final state. This is the object that we access when we run onDone in the parent (`likeImagesMachine`). If everything went well, you should be able to see the entire array of fetched images in your app right now. This is a good moment to run the app on your device or emulator if you haven't already.

Managing the image in the image modal

We have ourselves a nice setup—we're fetching images and feeding them to the app. Our app is rather static, though. We need a way to add new images to the liked images array. We would also like to check whether an image is liked so that we can display the proper icon in `ImageDetailsModal`.

If we want to know whether an image should be liked or unliked, we first need to know whether it's liked. But even before we can know whether an image has been liked, we need to know all the data pertinent to that image. We will add a new item to the context of the `likeImagesMachine` machine—`currentImage`:

```
export const likeImagesMachine  = createMachine({
  id: "likeImagesMachine ",
  context: {
    likedImages: [],
    currentImage: null,
  },
//…
```

This is where we will store information on the currently viewed image. The context is initialized as `null`, and we need to add an action that will update this context value. We will add a new event called `MODAL_OPEN` to the `ready` state of `likeImagesMachine`:

```
// src/machines/likeImagesMachine
ready: {
    on: {
      MODAL_OPEN: {
        actions: assign((context, event) => {
          return {
            currentImage: event.payload,
          };
        }),
      },
      MODAL_CLOSE: {
        actions: assign((context, event) => {
          return {
            currentImage: null,
          };
        }),
      },
```

```
      },
//…
```

We will call the MODAL_OPEN action when ImageDetailsModal is opened, and MODAL_CLOSE when the modal is closed—pretty straightforward! You can see the code in action here:

```
// src/surfaces/ImageDetailsModal.js
export const ImageDetailsModal = ({ navigation, route }) => {
  const globalServices = useXStateContext();
  const { send } = globalServices.likedImagesAppService;

  useEffect(() => {
    send({
      type: "MODAL_OPEN",
      payload: route.params.imageItem,
    });
    return () => {
      send("MODAL_CLOSE", {});
    };
  }, []);
```

We start by using a custom hook called useXStateContext in order to consume context values that we set up previously. Then, we use the send function from likedImagesAppService. Finally, I've added a useEffect hook calling the MODAL_OPEN action when the modal is rendered and MODAL_CLOSE as a cleanup function.

Now that we have the current image saved in the machine context, we can check whether it's liked or not. To do that, we will use yet another utility from XState: a custom hook called useSelector. **Selector** is a name that may sound familiar to you. In JavaScript, there are query selectors, Redux promotes using selector functions, and there are also CSS selectors. XState selectors are the closest ideologically to the ones in Redux. They are special functions that receive the current state and can return a value based on some conditions. Our current state is the array of images and the current image, and the condition is if the current image is in the image array. The code is illustrated in the following snippet:

```
const isImageLikedSelector = (state) => {
  if (!state.context.currentImage) {
    return;
  }
  const checkIfInImagesArray = state.context.likedImages.find(
```

```
        (image) => image.itemId === state.context.currentImage.
          itemId
  );


  return !!checkIfInImagesArray;
};
```

As mentioned previously, this selector will receive the current state as the first argument. We start by checking that the images array is not `null`. We are running a `find` function on that array, and if it were `null` or `undefined`, this would cause the app to crash. Once we're sure the images array exists, we can filter it by the current image. You can place this function anywhere you'd like (in the same file as the machine, in a file called `selectors` or `utilities`, and so on) and then import it into `ImageDetailsModal`:

```
// src/surfaces/ImageDetailsModal.js
export const ImageDetailsModal = ({ navigation, route }) => {
  const globalServices = useXStateContext();
  const { send } = globalServices.globalAppService;
  const isImageLiked = useSelector(
    globalServices.globalAppService,
    isImageLikedSelector
  );
```

The `isImageLiked` constant can be used in the component to check which icon should be displayed and which action (liking or unliking) should be called.

Liking images

Our state machines are aware of the array of images we have fetched and that we display on the `FavoritedImages` surface. They also become aware of the currently seen image through the `MODAL_OPEN` action. Now, we need to tell them what to do if someone presses the "like" button. Let's add a new action to the `likeImagesMachine` function:

```
// src/machines/likeImagesMachine.js
//...
ready: {
    on: {
      LIKE: {
        actions: assign((context, event) => {
          const updateImageArray = event.payload.
```

```
concat(context.likedImages);

        return {
          likedImages: updateImageArray,
        };
      }),
    },
//...
```

We're using the assigner function, which we've met before. Inside it, we're concatenating the array containing only the current image to the full array of all images. This way, the newly added image will be at the top of the array and at the top of `FlatList`. Now that the action is ready, we can call it in the modal, like so:

```
// src/surfaces/ImageDetailsModal
//...
<Pressable
        onPress={() => {
          if (!isImageLiked) {
            send({ type: "LIKE", payload:
              [route.params.imageItem] });
          }
//...
```

We've done quite a few changes—let's test them in our app. If you followed along, you should be able to see that the fetched images load correctly on the `FavoritedImages` surface. The `ImageDetails` modal opens correctly as well, showing a full heart for images that are liked and an empty heart for images that are not liked (those on the `Feed` surface). We can even press the empty heart and it changes to be filled! The like action and the selector work as expected! Great!

Unfortunately, `FlatList` is a little more stubborn. As mentioned before, `FlatList` needs explicit data changes in order to re-render, and we need it to re-render if we want to see the new images added. We will have to "twist its hand" a little bit, by adding this `useEffect` hook:

```
// src/components/ListOfFavorites
export const ListOfFavorites = ({ navigation }) => {
  const globalServices = useXStateContext();
  const [state] = useActor(globalServices.globalAppService);
  const [imageData, updateImageData] = useState([]);
```

```
useEffect(() => {
  updateImageData(state.context.likedImages);
}, [state.context.likedImages]);
//...
```

And now, everything should work flawlessly! Time for a pat on the back! We've covered a lot of topics in this section. We have gone over a real-world implementation of setting up multiple state machines, invoking fetching functions, passing context values between machines, calling actions, and using selectors. With this knowledge, you should be able to configure any app to use XState as the state management library.

Summary

XState is the first state management library in this book to be fundamentally based on mathematical principles. We talked briefly about those principles, as understanding them is very useful for understanding XState. The most important concept is state machines. They are not new in the world of mathematics; they are quite novel, however, when it comes to how we think about global state in mobile apps. Once we had a grasp on the theory and we discovered the very useful XState visualizer, we were ready to do real work. We set up XState in the Funbook app, using best practices described in the XState documentation. We covered the topic of implementing XState as the global state solution for the use case of managing liked images. We looked at fetching data and changing data with XState. I hope you enjoyed it! Now, it's time to continue our journey to the next outlier in the state management libraries world: **Jotai**.

Further reading

- `https://brilliant.org/wiki/finite-state-machines/`: Finite state machines.

- `https://www.w3.org/TR/scxml/`: W3C SCXML specification.

- `https://xstate.js.org/docs/recipes/react.html#local-state`: XState recipes.

- `https://xstate.js.org/docs/guides/context.html#assign-action`: Assigner action.

8

Integrating Jotai in a React Native App

In the previous chapter, we ventured into the mathematical world of **XState**. We will continue our journey by exploring another young state management library called **Jotai**. **Jotai** is inspired by an experimental state management library created at **Facebook** called Recoil. In this chapter, we will take a brief look at **Recoil**, an experimental state management library created by Facebook. Once we're comfortable with the main ideas of this library, namely a new concept called an "atomic state", we will take a deep dive into **Jotai**. We will configure Jotai in our app, and we'll continue to work on data fetching and managing liked images with the help of **Jotai**. Here's what we will go over in this chapter:

- What is **Recoil** and an atomic state?
- What is **Jotai**?
- Configuring **Jotai** in the Funbook app
- Using **Jotai** for `FavoritedImages`

By the end of this chapter, you will have a new way of looking at global state management – by dividing it into small items, called **atoms**. You will also know how to set up **Jotai** in a new project, and how to use it for data fetching and data management.

Technical requirements

In order to follow along with this chapter, you will need some knowledge of **JavaScript** and **ReactJS**. If you have followed at least *Chapters 1 to 4* of this book, you should be able to proceed without any issues.

Feel free to use an IDE of your choice, as **React Native** does not need any specific functionality. Currently, the most popular IDEs for frontend developers are Microsoft's VSCode, Atom, Sublime Text, and WebStorm.

The code snippets provided in this chapter are here to illustrate what we should be doing with the code. They do not provide the whole picture. To code along easier, please open the GitHub repo in your IDE and look at the files in there. You can either start with the file in the folder named `example-app-full` or `chapter-8`. If you start with `example-app-full`, you will be responsible for implementing the solutions described in this chapter. If you choose to look at `chapter-8`, you will see the entire solution implemented by me.

If you get stuck or lost, you can check the code in the GitHub repo: `https://github.com/PacktPublishing/Simplifying-State-Management-in-React-Native/tree/main/chapter-8`.

What is Recoil and an atomic state?

If you've been following this book chapter by chapter, you may be feeling as though the list of different types of state management libraries is never-ending. You would be right, to some extent. New state management libraries pop up every few weeks; they are sometimes purely open source, and sometimes company-backed. However, they rarely propose groundbreaking solutions. More often than not, they are newer implementations of known concepts. Those implementations are greatly appreciated, as every developer likes working comfortably – and what are those known concepts, you may ask?

There's a consensus in the **ReactJS** world that state management libraries can be divided into three types:

1. Flux type – these are state management libraries that hold the state outside of components and use a unidirectional data flow. They are inspired by **Facebook's Flux**, the most famous example being **Redux**. There are modern implementations of this flow, such as **Redux Toolkit** or **Zustand**.

2. Proxy type – these libraries "wrap" the state, conceptually similar to what a proxy does. When using this type of state management, the developer can subscribe to, and read, wrapped values like any other values in the component. The best examples of proxy-type state management are **React's Context**, **MobX**, or **Valtio**.

3. Atomic type – this is the state set at the lowest level, managed naturally by `setState` in class components and the `useState` hook in function components. Values set in this way can be passed around the app and used in a bigger context. **Facebook** created an experimental library to promote this type of state management, called **Recoil**. **Jotai** soon followed suit.

Recoil was created around mid-2020 and quickly garnered lots of attention. It was published by Facebook itself, the creators of React, so everyone was expecting a great new solution. The idea of using the smallest possible denomination of pieces of state, peppered and accessible throughout **React** apps, was enticing. Unfortunately, after the first gasp of excitement, a big part of the React community lost interest in **Recoil** and went about their days continuing to work mostly with Redux. Two years later, **Recoil's** documentation still states that it's experimental and few people are talking about it.

A small community of developers was paying more attention than the rest of us though. *Poimandres*, an open source developer collective, went to work and created their implementation of an atomic state. They called it **Jotai**. If you visit their GitHub page, you will see they also developed **Valtio**, a proxy-type state management library, and **Zustand**, a lightweight flux-type state management library. **Valtio** and **Zustand** are so far in the shadow of their more famous alternatives, but **Jotai** has dominated the stage for atomic state management. This library is production-ready; it's being actively developed through **GitHub**, and its developers provide constant support on an open Discord server. This is why we will talk about **Jotai**, and not **Recoil**, in this chapter.

What is Jotai?

As mentioned in the previous section, **Jotai** is an atomic-type state management library, created by a developer named *Daishi Kato*, as part of the *Poimandres* open source developer collective. I asked Daishi Kato a few questions through Twitter, and he was nice enough to answer me. The first question I had was why he decided to create **Jotai**. He said: "I have been creating various global state libraries, to eliminate necessity of memoizing selectors. One notable one is react-tracked, which is heavily depending on proxies. I noticed proxies don't work best for many cases and wanted another solution. **Recoil's** model is a best match for this. So, to solve my problem, I developed **Jotai**." As simple as that! He added that maintaining the various state management libraries he created takes about half of his time, leaving the rest to do freelance work. Daishi said he likes working most with **Jotai** and **Valtio** as they have unique features. "**Zustand** is valuable for being minimal. It's almost nothing. Likewise, react-tracked is still valuable providing minimal features." – Daishi added. When I asked how he would categorize state management libraries, he said he would divide them into two groups: keeping the state internal (as with `useState`) or externally. Daishi is continually working on new things; you can observe all his work in the *Jotai Labs* **GitHub** repo: `https://github.com/jotai-labs`. He's also interested in developing features for fetching and **React's Suspense**. You can find more links to his projects in the *Further reading* section.

We now have a good understanding of why Jotai was created. It aims to solve state management problems from a new perspective, following React's best practices and concepts proposed by the experimental Recoil library. It's time we try this "atomic" state approach in our app. Let's get to coding!

Configuring Jotai in the Funbook app

If you're a fan of simplicity, my dear reader, you may just fall in love with this state management library. Configuring it in our app only requires running the `install` command in the terminal:

```
npm install jotai
```

Alternatively, see the following:

```
Yarn add jotai
```

There's one hidden gem of configuration to be added: Suspense. I specifically used the word gem because this configuration requirement of **Jotai** will make your app crash less. Suspense is a new ReactJS functionality, created to only be able to render components that are ready to be rendered. As with any new functionality, the users need to get used to it, and sometimes need to be forced to try it. **Jotai** is doing exactly this: forcing the users to use Suspense, for their own good! Let's go ahead and add it at the root of our app:

```js
// ./App.js
import React, { useState, Suspense } from "react";

export default function App() {
//...

  if (!fontsLoaded) {
    return <AppLoading />;
  }

  return (
    <SafeAreaProvider>
//...
            <Suspense fallback={<AppLoading />}>
              <NavigationContainer theme={MyTheme}>
                <Stack.Navigator>
//...
```

Now, our app can use **Jotai**'s atoms and it's less prone to unexpected crashes. Let's move on to using atoms for ListOfFavoritedImages.

Using Jotai for ListOfFavoritedImages

You may have noticed that we didn't give much of a theoretical introduction to **Jotai**. This is because this library is minimal. There is no boilerplate, no complex concepts. All we need to do is create an atom and use it thanks to a custom hook in the app. Let's start by creating an atom with some mock data for the liked images:

```js
// src/atoms/imagesAtoms.js
import { atom } from "jotai";

export const imageListAtom = atom([
```

```
  {
    "itemId": 1,
    "authorId": 11,
    "timeStamp": "2 hrs ago",
    "url": "…",
    "likes": "28",
    "conversations": "12"
  },
  {
    "itemId": 2,
    "authorId": 7,
    "timeStamp": "1 week ago",
    "url": "…",
    "likes": "8",
    "conversations": "123"
  },
]);
```

We have the mocked images array ready; all we need to do now is use it. Given our previous experiences with other state management libraries, you are probably expecting to see some sort of setup, wrapper, subscription, or something similar. I'm sorry to disappoint, but all we need to do to use the **Jotai** atom is… use it. Let's change the code in the `ListOfFavoritedImages` component as follows:

```
import { useAtom } from "jotai";
import { imageListAtom } from "../atoms/imagesAtoms";

export const ListOfFavorites = ({ navigation }) => {
  const [imageList] = useAtom(imageListAtom);

  if (!imageList) {
    return <AppLoading />;
  }

//…
  return (
    //…
      <FlatList
```

```
          data={imageList}
//...
```

In the preceding code, we imported the **Jotai** custom hook named `useAtom` and the atom we created in our `imagesAtom` file. And what is the result? Let's run the app in the simulator and find out!

Figure 8.1 – App displaying images based on Jotai atoms

Everything works! I must admit, this feels almost magical. Surely, fetching will be more complicated?

Fetching data with Jotai

We successfully set up mocked image data in our app, but we would like to fetch real data from the server. Going back to the **Jotai** docs, we will find a guide on asynchronous atoms (you can find a link to this part of the documentation in the *Further reading* section). Here's what our async atom for fetching images will look like:

```
// src/atoms/imageAtoms.js
import { requestBase } from "../utils/constants";
import { atom } from "jotai";


export const imageListAtom = atom([]);
```

```
    const urlAtom = atom(requestBase + "/john_doe/likedImages.
       json");
export const fetchImagesAtom = atom(async (get) => {
    const response = await fetch(get(urlAtom));
    return await response.json();
});
```

We add a `requestBase` import to use URLs more comfortably. Then, we proceed to create a basic atom with the specific URL. The last function is the async atom. We know it's async because it uses the `async` keyword. The body of the async atom function is a `fetch` function and data return. The atom is ready, but it's not connected to anything just yet. We will need to call it in the app and make it fill `imageListAtom`. Let's start by invoking the fetching. A good place to do so will be at the root of the app once the user is logged in. This means we will not be fetching in the `App.js` root component, but rather in the `Home` component:

```
// src/surfaces/Home.js
import { useAtom } from "jotai";
import { fetchImagesAtom } from "../atoms/imageAtoms";
//...
export const Home = () => {
    const [json] = useAtom(fetchImagesAtom);
```

We start by importing the necessary pieces: a custom hook from **Jotai** and our fetching atom. Then, we use the hook in the component. This is a good moment to check that everything is working correctly. I suggest adding a `console.log` to the component and seeing whether the value of `json` is the same as expected. By the way, there is no rule for naming the returns of atoms. You may as well write this:

```
const [thisIsAVeryFancyAndCuteFetchingMechanism] =
    useAtom(fetchImagesAtom);
```

If you're using linter plugins (such as **ESLint**) in your IDE, you may have received a warning about the `json` value being declared but not used. What good does it do to fetch images if we're not doing anything with them? And what should we do with them? We should make the newly fetched array of images fill `imageListAtom`. The way to accomplish this is to change our read-only `imageListAtom` to a read-write atom.

Reading and writing atoms

Ah! Finally, some theory! I'm sure you've been craving this, my dear reader! (Since it's difficult to convey irony in a technical text, let me take this opportunity to explain: the previous sentence is sarcastic).

There are three types of atoms: read-only, write-only, and read-write atoms. The read-only atoms are the simplest: all you do is create them and set the value they need to hold on to, for example:

```
const onlyReadMe = atom('I like to read')
```

Read-only atoms can hold more than simple values or strings. If you need more complex logic in your atom, you should use the following syntax:

```
const readMeButInUpperCase  = atom((get) =>
    get(onlyReadMe).toUpperCase())
```

In the preceding short snippet, you can observe that atoms have access to a `getter` function, which, in turn, can access other atoms.

If we wanted to add a write functionality to our atom, we can add a `setter` function as the second argument to the atom:

```
const readMeButInUpperCase  = atom(
      (get) => get(onlyReadMe).toUpperCase(),
      (get, set, newText) => {
          set(onlyReadMe, newText)
      }
)
```

We've added a new function, which will accept a new text and pass it to the `onlyReadMe` atom. If you were to use it in a component, it would look like this:

```
const FancyTextComponent = () => {
    const [fancyText, setFancyText] =
    useAtom(readMeButInUpperCase  );

return (
      <Pressable onPress={() => setFancyText
        ('I do not like to swim')>
        <Text>Likes and dislikes: {fancyText}</Text>
    </Pressable>
)
```

In the example component in the preceding screenshot, you can observe how a read-write atom can be implemented. We start by importing the atom, but we declare two values: the value and the setter, very similar to what we would use in a regular `useState` hook. Lower in the component, we use {fancyText} to display the text from the atom, and the setFancyText function to set a new text through a button press.

The last type of atom we can talk about is the write-only atom. The only difference between this atom and a read-write atom is that we declare the read argument as null. Here's an example:

```
const onlyUsedForSettingValues  = atom(null,
    (get, set) => {
        set(onlyReadMe, 'I like using write only atoms')
    }
)
```

When using this type of atom, you always need to make sure to accommodate the hook with the non-existing default value. Here's how this write-only hook would be used in the preceding example component:

```
const FancyTextComponent = () => {
const [readOnlyFancyText] = useAtom(onlyReadMe);
    const [, setStaticText] =
      useAtom(onlyUsedForSettingValues  );

return (
    <Pressable onPress={() => setFancyText()>
        <Text>Likes and dislikes: { readOnlyFancyText }</Text>
    </Pressable>
)
```

Notice the comma in the array with values derived from the useAtom hook. It indicates there is a null value on the first index, but we choose to not use it.

Adding read-write functionality to the imageListAtom

So far, we have a read-only imageListAtom and an async fetchImagesAtom. Let's add a write functionality to imageListAtom so that it can accept values from fetchImagesAtom:

```
// src/atoms/imageAtoms.js
export const imageListAtom = atom([], (get, set, newArray) => {
  set(imageListAtom, newArray);
});
```

The atom is ready to receive values, so let's give it some. We have to go back to the Home component where we kicked off data fetching, and add a useEffect, which will update imageListAtom. Here's what the code should look like:

```
// src/surfaces/Home.js
export const Home = () => {
  const [json] = useAtom(fetchImagesAtom);
  const [, setAllImages] = useAtom(imageListAtom);

  useEffect(() => {
    if (json) {
      setAllImages(json);
    }
  }, [json]);
```

This is a good moment to check again whether everything works fine in the app since we just implemented data fetching. If everything is, in fact, working as expected, we'll move on to implementing functionality for the **Like** button. If you run into any issues, start by using console.log to check that the atoms hold and return the values you are expecting them to have. If you continue to have issues, you can join the *Poimandres* Discord server (link in the *Further reading* section), where you'll find a **Jotai**-dedicated channel. *Daishi Kato*, the author of **Jotai**, answers all sorts of questions on this channel himself.

Once you are sure that everything is good, we'll move on to implementing the **Like** button in ImageDetailsModal.

Implementing the Like button

The full functionality of the **Like** button in ImageDetailsModal consists of two parts: the heart icon being full or not – indicating whether the image has been liked, and the actual action of liking an image – which means adding the new image to the array of images on the Favorited surface.

Let's start by creating the necessary atom for the heart icon. We need to know whether a given image has been liked or not. We can establish whether it has been liked by filtering the array of images and checking whether a given image is present in the array. Here's what the resulting atom will look like:

```
// src/atoms/imageAtoms.js
  export const isImageLikedAtom = atom(false,
    (get, set, newImage) => {
```

```
   const imageList = get(imageListAtom);
   const checkIfLiked =
       imageList?.filter((favoritedImg) => favoritedImg.itemId
         === newImage.itemId)
       .length > 0;

   set(isImageLikedAtom, checkIfLiked);
});
```

As per the atom syntax, we start by establishing the default value as `false`. We then add a setter function, which will receive the new image object. Inside the setter function, we use **Jotai's** `get` function to get `imageListAtom` and check our current image object against it. Finally, we set `isImageLikedAtom` to the correct value. Once the atom is created, we need to use it in the component:

```
// src/surfaces/ImageDetailsModal.js
export const ImageDetailsModal = ({ navigation, route }) => {
    const [isCurrentImageLiked, setIsLiked] =
      useAtom(isImageLikedAtom);

  setIsLiked(route.params.imageItem);
//...
```

You may wonder why we are calling the `setIsLiked` function so crudely – why not add `useEffect`? The fact of the matter is that we need this function to be called when the component is rendered and only then. We could add a `useEffect` hook with an empty dependency array, but it would achieve the same result while looking more complicated.

When does it run?

There are some subtleties to the React component life cycle. They are more obvious with class components, where we would use `componentDidMount`, `componentWillUnmount`, and so on. Functional components have the same life cycle, without being as obvious about it. And it so happens that the `useEffect` hook only runs after a given component has finished rendering, while functions called directly do not wait for the render to finish.

As far as our example goes, we do not need to make sure the rendering is complete before calling the `setIsLiked` function. However, big applications often ask a lot of their developers, and you may face a case where you need to closely control when a given atom setter function (or any other function for that matter) is run. You can read more on this topic in *Difference between 'useEffect' and calling function directly inside a component*, linked in the *Further reading* section.

Circling back to our use case: we have a very nice `isImageLiked` atom in place. You can test that it works correctly by opening image modals on the **Feed** surface – where the heart icon should be empty – and on the **Favorites** surface – where the heart icon should be full.

Now, on to the liking action! We will not need to do anything too fancy here. We must take `imageListAtom` and add a new image to it:

```
// src/atoms/imageAtoms.js
export const addImageToArray = atom(
        null,
        (get, set, newImage) => {
          const clonedArray = get(imageListAtom);
          clonedArray.unshift(newImage);
          set(imageListAtom, clonedArray);
          set(isImageLikedAtom, newImage);
        }
);
```

As with the example write-only atom, we start by declaring a null for the default atom value. In the setter function, we get `imageListAtom` and we add the new image using the `unshift` function, which adds items to the beginning of the original array. We finish by setting the newly created array as `imageListAtom` and by triggering the setter in `isImageLikedAtom`. Let's add this to the modal component:

```
// src/surfaces/ImageDetailsModal.js
export const ImageDetailsModal = ({ navigation, route }) => {
  const [, addImage] = useAtom(addImageToArray);
  const [isCurrentImageLiked, setIsLiked] =
useAtom(isImageLikedAtom);

  setIsLiked(route.params.imageItem);

return (
//...
    <Pressable
        onPress={() => {
```

```
          if (isCurrentImageLiked) {
            // add remove image functionality here
          } else {
            addImage(route.params.imageItem);
          }
        }}
      >

        <Ionicons name={isCurrentImageLiked ? "heart" :
          "heart-outline"} />
      </Pressable>
//...
```

We must import the `addImageToArray` atom into our component and then call it in the right place upon the button being tapped. Let's test our app! Chances are everything is working perfectly fine. You can tap the heart icon when it's empty and it becomes full, and when you close the modal and go to the **Favorites** surface, the image is present there. If you don't see the new image on the **Favorites** surface appear immediately, you may be facing an issue caused by `FlatList`.

React Native's `FlatList` is a pure component, which means it does not re-render unless specifically instructed to do so. We have encountered this same problem already when using **MobX**. In the case of **MobX**, we used special utilities to pass values to `FlatList`. **Jotai**, being minimal, does not offer these specialized utilities. We must manage this problem outside of **Jotai**. There are a few things we can do. We can try using the `extraData` prop from `FlatList` – we can pass atom values to `useState` and let the natural state re-render the component. We can also take advantage of the utilities provided by the React Navigation library. This is my favorite approach, and it is the one I chose to use. There's a `useIsFocused` custom hook in **React Navigation**, which can be used to force a re-render when a tab is focused. From this description, you can see that this is exactly what we need! Let's add this hook to the `Favorites` surface:

```
// src/surfaces/Favorites.js
import { useIsFocused } from "@react-navigation/native";

export const Favorites = ({ navigation }) => {
  const isFocused = useIsFocused();

  return (
      <SafeAreaView style={{ flex: 1, paddingTop: headerHeight
        }}>
      <Suspense fallback={<AppLoading />}>
        <ListOfFavorites navigation={navigation}
```

```
isFocused={isFocused} />
//...
```

Using this hook, the `Favorites` surface will re-render every time this tab is focused. Of course, this is a hook to be used with great caution. Too many re-renders cause apps to crash unexpectedly. If you do decide to use it, make sure the re-render is necessary.

Time to visit the Funbook app again! In this section, we started by using a basic hook with a mock array of images. We then implemented data fetching using **Jotai**. We learned about the three types of atoms: read-only, write-only, and read-write. We used all of this knowledge to create the **Like** button functionality with **Jotai** atoms. So, when you test your app, try using the **Like** button in `ImageDetailsModal` and check whether your images on the **Favorites** surface are updated correctly.

Summary

In this chapter, we covered **Jotai**, a new kid on the block of state management libraries. Inspired by a new, atomic approach to state management proposed by Facebook through their library named **Recoil**, **Jotai** has become more and more popular within the React community. It offers a bottom-up approach, as opposed to top-down libraries, such as **Redux** or **MobX**. It's honestly stupidly easy to configure and use. It doesn't offer many utilities, but the documentation is very clear and easy to use. In this chapter, we managed to use it to fetch and store data, and we also used it to implement actions on that data, such as adding items to an array. **Jotai** marks the end of our journey with classic state management libraries.

In the next chapter, we'll talk about **React Query**, which is not a state management library, but a data-fetching library. It does have its place in this book, however. More on that in the next chapter! See you there!

Further reading

- `https://marmelab.com/blog/2022/06/23/proxy-state-with-valtio.html`: A State Management Tour: Proxy State with Valtio.

- `https://github.com/facebookexperimental/Recoil/tree/main`: *Recoil* GitHub page.

- `https://opencollective.com/pmndrs`: Poimandres website.

- `https://github.com/dai-shi/react-suspense-fetch`: `react-suspense-fetch`.

- `https://github.com/dai-shi/react-hooks-fetch`: `react-hooks-fetch`.

- `https://github.com/dai-shi/react-hooks-worker`: `react-hooks-worker`.

- `https://jotai.org/docs/guides/async`: *Jotai – Async*.

- `https://discord.com/invite/poimandres`: Poimandres Discord server.

- `https://www.geekyhub.in/post/difference-between-useeffect-and-direct-function-call/`: *Difference between 'useEffect' and calling function directly inside a component.*

- `https://reactnavigation.org/docs/function-after-focusing-screen/#re-rendering-screen-with-the-useisfocused-hook`: React Navigation `useIsFocused` hook.

9

Using React Query for Server-Side-Driven State Management

Welcome, my dear reader, to the last chapter describing state management solutions for our Funbook app. In the previous chapter, we looked at the youngest state management library (as of the writing of this book) – **Jotai**. Jotai is a minimal solution, based on ideas proposed by the **Facebook** team in their open source library – **Recoil**. **React Query** is minimal as well but in a very different sense. React Query is created for managing fetching and mutating data on the server. In this chapter, we will look at what React Query has to offer. We will start by taking a broad look at this library; we will then implement it for data fetching. With our current app setup, we don't have a real backend server to communicate with, so we can only look at mutating data in theory. We will also look at a few specialized utilities created for **React Native** by the React Query team.

Here's a list of topics we will cover in this chapter:

- What is React Query and why is it in this book?
- Installing and configuring React Query
- Using React Query for data fetching
- Other React Query functionalities
- React Query utilities for React Native

By the end of this chapter, you will have a good understanding of how you can use React Query to improve your developer experience and your code bases. You will have a good knowledge of how to handle fetching data with React Query and a general knowledge of other functionalities of this library.

Technical requirements

In order to follow along with this chapter, you will need some knowledge of **JavaScript** and **ReactJS**. If you have followed at least *Chapters 1* through *4* of this book, you should be able to go forward without any issues.

Feel free to use an IDE of your choice, as **React Native** does not need any specific functionality. Currently, the most popular IDEs for frontend developers are Microsoft's VSCode, Atom, Sublime Text, and WebStorm.

The code snippets provided in this chapter are here to illustrate what we should be doing with the code. They do not provide the whole picture. For a better experience while coding alongside reading this chapter, please open the GitHub repo in your IDE and look at the files in there. You can either start with the files in the folder named `example-app-full` or `chapter-9` If you start with `example-app-full` you will be responsible for implementing the solutions described in this chapter. If you choose to look at `chapter-9` you will see the entire solution implemented by me.

If you get stuck or lost, you can check the code in the GitHub repo: `https://github.com/PacktPublishing/Simplifying-State-Management-in-React-Native/tree/main/chapter-9`.

What is React Query and why is it in this book?

First things first: let's talk about the name of this library. In this chapter, I use the name React Query, it is also a commonly used name. However, the creator of React Query, *Tanner Linsley*, did some restructuring in 2022, in the open source libraries that he owns and maintains. He created an umbrella name, **TanStack**, and placed a plethora of libraries under this name. And so, React Query became TanStack Query, as of React Query version 4. You can find a link to the TanStack home page in the *Further reading* section at end of this chapter.

Now that we have the name out of the way, let's talk about the place of React Query in this book. React Query is *not* a state management library. It's a library offering a solution for comfortable fetching and data mutations on the server. Why are we talking about it then? Because it turns out that efficient communication with the server can replace any need for global state management. Given our real-life social media app clone, we've been managing liked images in every chapter. What if, instead of working with the app state, every time a user likes an image, we sent that information to the server? Or when the user visits the **FavoritedImages** surface we pull the latest version of the list from the server? You may think: "Boy, that would be a lot of requests! A lot of loading states and the app being useless…" And you would be right! Except if you use React Query. React Query not only facilitates data fetching, but it also manages cached values, refreshing values, background fetching, and much more.

Now that we have a theoretical understanding of what React Query is, we can get to coding. Let's play with this non-state-management library.

Installing and configuring React Query

Installing this library is no different from any other dependency, we need to run an installation script. To do this using npm, enter the following:

```
$ npm i @tanstack/react-query
```

Or if you would prefer to use yarn, enter the following:

```
$ yarn add @tanstack/react-query
```

Once the library is installed, we will need to add some minimal boilerplate. We will need to let our app know that we're using React Query. We will need to use a special wrapper. Do you see where I'm going with this? Yes! We will use a provider as follows:

```js
// App.js
import {
  QueryClient,
  QueryClientProvider,
} from '@tanstack/react-query'
//…

const queryClient = new QueryClient()

export default function App() {
//…
  return (
    <SafeAreaProvider>
    <QueryClientProvider client={queryClient}>
//…
      </QueryClientProvider>
    </SafeAreaProvider>
  );
}
//…
```

We will start by importing the necessary functions from React Query – QueryClient and QueryClientProvider. Then, we will create a new QueryClient function and pass it to QueryClientProvider. Our app is ready to use React Query functionalities instead of simple fetching.

This is a good moment to make sure the app is running correctly on your simulator or device.

Once you have made sure installing new dependencies did not break anything unexpected in your project, we will be ready to implement real data fetching with React Query in the next section.

Using React Query for data fetching

As you know, we need to fetch a few different pieces of data for our app. We will fetch a list of avatars, a list of images for the feed surface, a list of images for the `FavoritedImages` surface, and a list of conversations. We are free to add the React Query fetching wherever we like. For simple queries, we can simply use the `useQuery` hook provided by the library in our components. We can also write our own custom hooks, holding more logic or conditions. Let's start by looking at the simplest possible example: querying the server to check whether the user is logged in.

In order to use a React Query hook in the top-level component where we set up our navigation to display either the login screen or not, we will need to reorganize our code a little bit. We cannot have `QueryClientProvider` in the return statement of the same component trying to use a `useQuery` hook. Let's change the name of the main component from `App` to `AppWrapped` and let's add this new app component in the `App.js` file:

```
// App.js
export default function App() {
    return (
        <QueryClientProvider client={queryClient}>
        <AppWrapped />
        </QueryClientProvider>
    )
};
```

Now, let's change the name of the main component from `App` to `AppWrapped`, and let's remove `QueryClientProvider` from the child component. Let me remind you that if you ever get lost in the code examples, you can take a look at the GitHub repo: `https://github.com/PacktPublishing/Simplifying-State-Management-in-React-Native/tree/main/chapter-9`.

Our `AppWrapped` component should be ready to use the `useQuery` hook. Make sure you start by importing it as follows:

```
// App.js
import {
  useQuery,
//...
```

```
} from '@tanstack/react-query'

//…
const fetchLoginStatus = async () => {
    const response = await fetch(requestBase +
      "/loginState.json");
    return response.json();
  }



const AppWrapped = () => {
  const { data } = useQuery(['loginState'],
    fetchLoginStatus);
//…
{!data?.loggedIn ? (
    <Stack.Screen name='Login' component={Login} />
        ) : (
        <>
            <Stack.Screen
            name='Home'
//…
```

After you've imported the useQuery hook, you need to create a function responsible for fetching and awaiting data from the server. This is the fetchLoginStatus function, which we will pass to the useQuery hook. This function can be created in any file you would like. Once we have the fetching set up, we need to use the useQuery hook in the component. We pull in a destructured object key data, where we check the loggedInStatus value.

> **Object destructuring**
>
> Depending on how often you use modern JavaScript, you may have noticed the destructuring syntax, where the const keyword is followed by items in curly or square brackets. This syntax is called destructuring assignment and is used to unpack values from arrays (square brackets), objects, or properties (curly brackets).
>
> const { data } = objectWithADataItem is the same as const data = objectWithADataItem.data.

Now that we have seen a simple example, let's look at something slightly more complex and create a custom hook and a dependent query.

Fetching image data

Fetching image data could be just as simple as fetching the login state data; however, I would like to talk about something more complicated. So, we will artificially complicate our lives by making sure the images are fetched only after the user is logged in. We will start by creating a custom hook called useCustomImageQuery inside a newly created queries folder. Our custom hook will return a useQuery hook:

```
// src/queries/useCustomImageQuery
import { useQuery } from "@tanstack/react-query";
import { requestBase } from "../utils/constants";

const getImages = async () => {
  const response = await fetch(requestBase +
    "/john_doe/likedImages.json");
  return response.json();
}

export const useCustomImageQuery = () => {
  const { data } = useQuery(['loginState']);

  return useQuery(
    ["imageList"],
    getImages,
    {
    enabled: data?.loggedIn,
  });
};
```

We started by importing the necessary useQuery function and our utility requestBase. Next, we created our fetching function called getImages. This function fetches data from a given API endpoint and returns it. Finally, we created a custom hook called useCustomImageQuery. On the first line of the hook, we check the loginState query. It looks different than in App.js where we used it first, doesn't it? It has only one parameter: loginState. This parameter is called a **query key** in the React Query world and it is literally a key to unlocking the power of React Query. Using this key, you can access any and all previously fetched data; you could also invalidate it manually or mutate it. As for us, we only need to check the login status now, using this particular query key.

The `return` statement of our custom hook consists of a `useQuery` hook with three parameters. In the first place, we have the awesomely important query key, `imageList`. Next, we see the call to the fetching function. Last but not least, we have a configuration object holding a key called `enabled`. This key determines when the given query should be called. In our case, the query will be called when the result of the `loginStatus` query returns the value of `true`. We just successfully set up React Query to fetch images. All that is left is to display them. Let's go to the `ListOfFavorited` component where we will replace the context call with the following custom hook:

```js
// src/components/ListOfFavorited.js
import { useCustomImageQuery } from "../queries/
  useCustomImageQuery";
//…
export const ListOfFavorites = ({ navigation }) => {
  const { data: queriedImages } = useCustomImageQuery();

//…
  return (
//…
    <FlatList
    data={ queriedImages }
//…
```

If everything went according to plan, you should be able to run the application now and see a list of favorited images, which is pulled by React Query from the backend. If you run into any trouble, remember that the custom hook we created is just another function, and can be debugged as such. You can put `console.log` in the component, in the hook, or in the `getImages` function called by the hook.

Hopefully, you were able to set up everything smoothly. In this section, we practiced using React Query for fetching and displaying data. We leveraged ReactJS knowledge – because we created a custom hook – but React Query hooks can be set up in many ways. Given that our app has a fake backend that can only serve data, this is as far as we can go in practical usage of React Query. I invite you though, my dear reader, to continue reading and find out what other great functionalities this library holds.

Other React Query Functionalities

As stated above, we can't use React Query in our example app to mutate data on the server because our backend is not robust enough. In a real-life application, you would most probably use an API that accepts a POST request just as well as a GET request. In these cases, you would be able to change data with the help of React Query. In order to do so, we are provided with another specialized hook: useMutation. Here's what this hook would look like if we could use it for the favorited images:

```
const imageListMutation = useMutation(newImage => {
  return fetch('/john_doe/likedImages ',
    {method: 'POST', body: newImage})
});
```

The preceding function is very simple. It wraps a fetch call in a React Query utility. This utility offers us a few things, such as the fact that it has the following states: isIdle, isLoading, isError, and isSuccess. We can check these states and update the view accordingly. We would use this mutation in ImageDetailsmodal:

```
// src/surfaces/ImageDetailsmodal.js
//...
export const ImageDetailsmodal = ({ navigation }) => {
  const imageListMutation = useMutation(newImage => {
    return fetch('/john_doe/likedImages ',
      {method: 'POST', body: newImage})
  });
//...
  return (
//...
      <Pressable
        onPress={() => {
          imageListMutation.mutate({route.params.imageItem
            })
        }}
      >
      {mutation.isLoading ? (
        <Text>Loading...</Text>
          ) : (
            <Ionicons
              //...
```

```
        /> )
        }
    </Pressable>
//…
```

Let me reiterate: we are doing a dry run of sending data to the server because our app's backend cannot handle a `POST` request.

In the preceding code, we started by adding a React Query mutation function to `ImageDetailsModal`. We passed it into the `Pressable` component. Then, inside the `Pressable` component, we added a ternary operator to check whether the mutation is in a loading state. In case it is, we display a `Text` component saying **Loading…**. This is a minimal example of how you can take advantage of mutation states. In a real-world app, you would probably check for `isSucccess` and `isError` as well and you would probably handle loading more gracefully.

This is all nice, but the way we implemented the mutation above we would still need to re-fetch the data traditionally to have the latest version in the `ListOfFavorites` component. Unless, we use the full power of React Query and update the cached version of data, fetched previously through the `useCustomImageQuery` hook! Here's what we would need to change in the mutation:

```
const updateImges = () => {
    return fetch('/john_doe/likedImages ',
        {method: 'POST', body: newImage})
}

const imageListMutation = useMutation(updateImges, {
    onSuccess: data => {
        queryClient.setQueryData(['imageList'], data)
    }
})
```

In the preceding code snippet, we started by extracting the `fetch` function for better readability. We then add `onSuccess` logic to the mutation and we tell it to update the item marked by the `imageList` query key with the new data. Thanks to this strategy we will not have to manually update the `imageList` data every time a mutation occurs. You can read more about updating after mutation responses in the TanStack documentation, linked in the *Further reading* section.

We have covered the two most important aspects of React Query: fetching and mutating data. However, there's much more functionality to be taken advantage of in a real-life project. You can check the fetching status, just like we did with the example mutation. You can also do parallel queries for fetching data simultaneously. If you want to, you can set initial data to fill your views before fetching is complete.

It is also possible to pause or disable queries whenever you need. For large datasets, there is a special type of query, a paginated query, which will batch data into consumable chunks. In case your data is infinite, React Query provides utilities for infinite queries. Many big apps may take advantage of prefetching data on page load.

I encourage you, my dear reader, to read the React Query documentation to be able to grasp all the possible solutions it offers. I was surprised myself while using React Query by how many common problems are solved out of the box by this library.

React Query utilities for React Native

As we all know, React Native has its own quirks as compared to pure ReactJS. React Query doesn't leave managing those quirks to the developers, but rather steps up with some interesting solutions. For example, there's an `onlineManager` that can be added to React Native apps to have our apps reconnect when they are online. If we would like to refresh or refetch data when the app is focused, we can use React Query's `focusManager` together with React Native's `AppState`. In some cases, we may want to refetch data when a specific screen in our app is focused, and React Query offers a solution for that use case as well. If you want to read about these utilities and how to use them in more detail, head over to the TanStack documentation at `https://tanstack.com/query/v4/docs/react-native`.

Summary

React Query is battle tested for scaling applications and can be a great solution for all sorts of projects. In this chapter, we installed it in the Funbook app and added it to the app. We didn't configure anything specific, as our project is small and didn't require any changes from the default configuration. We then looked at how a simple data fetching mechanism can be used for checking the login status of the user. Next, we created and used another, more complex, data-fetching hook with a dependency. We displayed the fetched data and then we took a tour of other React Query utilities. React Query is the last stop in our journey through the world of state management libraries for React Native apps. I hope you enjoyed the ride!

I invite you, my dear reader, to accompany me to the last chapter, where we will summarize everything we have learned on the topic of state management in React Native apps.

Further reading

- `https://tanstack.com/` – The TanStack home page.
- `https://tanstack.com/query/v4/docs/guides/updates-from-mutation-responses` – TanStack Query, *Updates from Mutation Responses*.

Part 4 – Summary

In this part, readers will get an overview of all the different solutions covered throughout the book.
This part includes the following chapter:

- *Chapter 10, Appendix*

10
Appendix

Well, my dear reader, we have reached the last part of this book: the summary. I sincerely hope you enjoyed reading what I had to say about state management libraries in **React Native** and I want to thank you for getting this far. Let me take you now on a trip down memory lane of everything we talked about in this book. And if afterward you're not too tired of my thoughts and ruminations, you will find a bonus section on recruitment interview questions related to **state management**.

In the first chapters of this book, we looked very broadly at the history of web development. We saw the evolution of the internet landscape, which led to the creation of **ReactJS**. Then, we talked about the evolution of **React** itself, which led to the creation of React Native. Knowing how close React Native is to ReactJS can be of great help while working on React Native apps. The ReactJS community is bigger and more mature than its mobile-first cousin. Many issues that React Native developers face can be solved with ReactJS knowledge. There's a notion called the **React mindset**, which is crucial for writing robust, scalable, and bug-free apps. There are many great articles on this topic, for example, the *Thinking in React* article posted inside the official React documentation. Once we learned how to adopt this mindset, we started building our very own app: Funbook.

Unsurprisingly, the app we created is a social media clone app. Social media apps are an interesting topic for example code, as most of us are very familiar with how they should work. At the same time, they are much more complicated than the traditional to-do app, present in most ReactJS tutorials. Setting up any mobile app is a task on its own. For all the web developers out there, working on mobile apps is new territory, with its own tooling and processes. Luckily, we can take advantage of **Expo**, and have a functioning and testable app in minutes. Once we got comfortable with the basic app setup, we got to coding the real Funbook app. We added a few surfaces: Feed, Conversations, Liked Images, and Camera. Then we got to think in React! We planned and wrote the underlying components of all the surfaces. We used many modern React features, such as hooks and context. By the end of *Chapter 4*, we had a beautiful, functioning mobile app, which we could test on real devices or on phone simulators on our computer screens. This may seem like a lot of work, but let me assure you: before React Native, and a few of its **JavaScript** predecessors, creating mobile apps working on **Android** and **iOS** was a lot more work!

*Chapter 5, Implementing Redux in Our Funbook App, w*as the first to talk about external solutions for state management in React Native apps. The specific solution we talked about was **Redux** and **Redux Toolkit**. Redux is the oldest and most widely known and used state management library in the React community, as of the time of writing this book. When used wisely, it's a great tool. It requires quite a bit of boilerplate, and its creator has doubts about how it's implemented. However, the team behind Redux Toolkit has made great progress in keeping this library developer-friendly and up to date. We configured Redux and Redux Toolkit in the Funbook app, and we saw how to use them for managing the list of liked images.

In the next chapter, we talked about a library considered to be the second most popular in the React community: **MobX**. By this time, we were armed with a sound knowledge of ReactJS, React Native, and some thoughts on how global state could be managed by React alone or with Redux. MobX invited us to rethink a few preconceptions and look at global state management differently. Instead of passing props or actions through an intricate web of components, MobX gives us tools to use global state data as any other prop, while only informing components about being observed. We learned later that this sort of global state management is sometimes called **proxy-based**. The state management library stands between the user and the code, managing state in a sort of invisible layer, like a proxy on the web. MobX is sometimes compared to **Valtio**, another proxy-based state management library.

After learning about MobX observables, actions, and their approach to deriving state values (which should be done as much as possible), we were ready to use it. We implemented the same functionality as for Redux – managing the list of liked images. And once we had that working in MobX, we moved on to the next state management library: **XState**.

Xstate is less popular than Redux and MobX, but it offers yet another way of looking at global state management. And even better, it offers a dedicated tool for doing so! The **Xstate visualizer** is an incredible tool that can be used for working in any global state for any app. Being able to see how different pieces of state relate to each other can come in handy when you're tasked with creating a new app. Xstate not only provides this great tool, but its creator invites us also to take a more mathematical approach to state management. Thanks to him, we can learn what a state machine is and that every part of the global state in an app should always be in a defined state.

After playing around with Xstate, and of course, implementing the list of liked images with it, we were ready to move on. The next library we looked at was **Jotai**.

Jotai was considered the new kid on the block when I started writing this book. That was many moons ago! As of the time of writing this summary, there are a few newer state management libraries. I feared they were not mature enough to be analyzed along with big players such as Redux and MobX. Jotai, however, has been holding strong over the last few months and getting more and more attention from the community. Jotai was heavily inspired by **Recoil**, a state management library created by the React team at Meta. Recoil remains in an experimental state, but Jotai is ready for usage in production apps.

The main concept in Jotai is the use of **atoms**. They are the smallest building block of global state that we can pepper around the app – just like we could pepper it with `useState` hooks. The big difference is that Jotai's atoms will be freely available throughout the app, without unpleasant prop drilling or extensive boilerplate. Using Jotai for the list of liked images felt, for me, a little bit magical: a minimal configuration and we can access pieces of state wherever we'd like!

Once we used Jotai in the Funbook app, we were ready to abandon it and move on to the next thing. And the next thing was very different from its predecessors – **React Query**, and the notion that we may not need any state management library at all. React Query is not a state management library; it's a library created for better data management and synchronization between an app and the server. It aims at reducing network calls while keeping data relevant. It is also an incredible solution as far as developer experience is concerned. The documentation is exhaustive, and it is accompanied by a specialized blog. Dozens of common developer problems are solved within the library itself. We used React Query, or **TanStack Query**, for fetching the list of liked images. We were, unfortunately, unable to use other features it offers, such as data mutations, as the backend of the Funbook app is quite minimal.

The creators of React Query ask a very good question: do you really need a state management library for your app? Let's ask ourselves this same question. We were able to create the Funbook app using React alone. We were also able to use React Query mixed with local state. Does this mean all dedicated state management libraries should be wiped from the earth along with this book? Certainly not.

Choosing a state management library, when choosing from battle-tested solutions, boils down to developer experience. The end user of your app will not know whether you're using Jotai or Redux, but your fellow developers may give you an earful about it. Some developers live and breathe Redux, while others would rather not touch Redux-based projects. There is a silent global consensus in the community that state management libraries should not be used for fetching and persisting data in apps. This task should be left for better-suited libraries, such as React Query. So, maybe the next app you create will use MobX for local state and React Query for fetching data? Or maybe Xstate for local state, **Axios** for fetching, and **Async Storage** for persisting state? Or maybe something else completely. I believe every state management library has its strong points, as well as weaknesses. I also believe discussing which is better is a moot point, as neither is objectively better. I hope that thanks to this book, you were able to "dip your toe" in a few different solutions and you are more aware of what you personally prefer. And once you find what you like, have fun working with it!

Bonus content

Speaking of work: you may find yourself , my dear reader, going through job interviews where you are asked about React, React Native, and state management solutions. There are a few questions I have gotten myself that I found were either very common or very interesting. I've compiled a list of those questions in the hope that they facilitate your next recruitment. Questions regarding React and Redux pop up in most job interviews for roles related to software development with React and React Native. Questions about other state management libraries may get asked if you specify that you are familiar with the given libraries. To be honest, 80% of job offers list React and Redux. I'm hoping this will change in the coming months and years, as other state management libraries offer great solutions. Here are some common or interesting questions:

1. In React, what is the difference between `props` and `state`?
2. Is it necessary to use an external state management library in a React Native app?
3. In Redux, what is a reducer and an action?
4. In Redux, what is the advantage of using selectors?
5. In Redux, are you allowed to change state values directly?
6. In MobX, what is a model?
7. In MobX, how do you make a component aware of the global state values?
8. In Xstate, what is a state machine?
9. In Xstate, how do you pass additional data through the state machine?
10. In Jotai, what is the name of the most basic piece of state?
11. Can you replace all state management with React Query alone?

I'm giving you only the questions because giving you the answers would be a tad too easy, don't you think? If you must go back in the book and research the answers, or maybe simply google them, there's a better chance the information will stick with you.

I sincerely hope you enjoyed reading this book just as much as I enjoyed writing it! Thank you for sticking around, and feel free to contact me through Twitter (if it still exists by the time this book gets published!). Good night and good luck!

Index

Hi!

I am Ola Desmurs-Linczewska, author of *Simplifying State Management in React Native*. I really hope you enjoyed reading this book and found it useful for learning about different state management solutions in React Native apps.

It would really help me (and other potential readers!) if you could leave a review on Amazon sharing your thoughts on *Simplifying State Management in React Native*.

Your review will help me to understand what's worked well in this book, and what could be improved upon for future editions, so it really is appreciated.

Best Wishes,
Aleks.

https://twitter.com/p_syche_

https://github.com/p-syche

https://adlinczewska.com/

Other Books You May Enjoy

If you enjoyed this book, you may be interested in these other books by Packt:

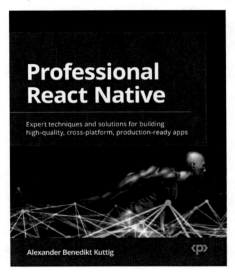

Professional React Native

Alexander Benedikt Kuttig

ISBN: 978-1-80056-368-1

- Become familiar with how React Native works under the hood
- Understand how to make the most of React Native for app development
- Explore different approaches to building apps across various platforms
- Become familiar with process automation and automated testing
- Contribute to open source code and structure your own code library
- Understand how to set up the architecture for bigger React Native projects

React and React Native - Fourth Edition

Adam Boduch, Roy Derks, Mikhail Sakhniuk

ISBN: 978-1-80323-128-0

- Explore React architecture, component properties, state, and context
- Work with React Hooks for handling functions and components
- Implement code splitting using lazy components and Suspense
- Build robust user interfaces for mobile and desktop apps using Material-UI
- Write shared components for Android and iOS apps using React Native
- Simplify layout design for React Native apps using NativeBase
- Write GraphQL schemas to power web and mobile apps
- Implement Apollo-driven components

Packt is searching for authors like you

If you're interested in becoming an author for Packt, please visit `authors.packtpub.com` and apply today. We have worked with thousands of developers and tech professionals, just like you, to help them share their insight with the global tech community. You can make a general application, apply for a specific hot topic that we are recruiting an author for, or submit your own idea.

Download a free PDF copy of this book

Thanks for purchasing this book!

Do you like to read on the go but are unable to carry your print books everywhere?

Is your eBook purchase not compatible with the device of your choice?

Don't worry, now with every Packt book you get a DRM-free PDF version of that book at no cost.

Read anywhere, any place, on any device. Search, copy, and paste code from your favorite technical books directly into your application.

The perks don't stop there, you can get exclusive access to discounts, newsletters, and great free content in your inbox daily

Follow these simple steps to get the benefits:

1. Scan the QR code or visit the link below

https://packt.link/free-ebook/9781803235035

2. Submit your proof of purchase
3. That's it! We'll send your free PDF and other benefits to your email directly

Made in the USA
Columbia, SC
20 January 2023

10790368R00113